THEY STOOD BOLDLY

By William P. Barker

TWELVE WHO WERE CHOSEN
KINGS IN SHIRTSLEEVES
PERSONALITIES AROUND JESUS
AS MATTHEW SAW THE MASTER
EVERYONE IN THE BIBLE
THEY STOOD BOLDLY

THEY STOOD BOLDLY

MEN AND WOMEN
IN THE BOOK OF ACTS

William P. Barker

FLEMING H. REVELL COMPANY
WESTWOOD, NEW JERSEY

Unless otherwise indicated, the Scripture quotations in this publication are from the *Revised Standard Version of the Bible,* copyrighted 1946 and 1952.

To friends in the Church of Christ in Thailand, who welcomed us as fellow workers, who blessed us with the privilege of serving Christ's church with them, and who gave us a new understanding of how the Holy Spirit works in the witnessing community.

A NOTE OF DEEP THANKS:

To Mrs. Howard E. Betts, Mrs. Neil N. Rennick, and Mrs. Fred F. Smoot for so carefully typing and proofreading; to John B. Barker, Frank S. Mead, Harry L. Norlander, Fred M. Rogers, and Sarah E. Wylie for their many helpful suggestions; to Mr. and Mrs. William E. Clark and the Bower Hill Community Church, United Presbyterian, for making possible a leave of absence during the summer of 1965 when much of this was written; to Jean, Jock, and Ellen for their interest and encouragement.

PREFACE

Before going into a foreign country, it is helpful to do some reading about the place. A few hours with a good guidebook shows us what to see and helps us avoid the exasperating waste of time and energy that so many inexperienced tourists encounter.

The Bible, for most of us, is a foreign continent. In a journey through the strange territory in the Book of Acts, a guidebook is helpful.

This book is meant to be such a guidebook. It is not an exhaustive volume covering everything there is to be known about Acts. It simply directs attention to the most important points of interest.

No guidebook can ever take the place of the excitement of an actual visit to the foreign country. Neither can this book be a substitute for the thrill of actually reading Acts. As with any guidebook, it is intended primarily to stimulate enough interest in the place described to make the reader journey there himself.

Without getting bogged down in a dreary desert of facts, let's take a minute to get our bearings. Who wrote Acts? Why? When?

The author was Luke, the writer of the third Gospel account. He was a physician (see Colossians 4:14), a highly educated man, probably a graduate of one of the great universities of the ancient world, a Gentile and not a Jew. He probably never saw Jesus but was an early convert. Some scholars think that Luke was a native of Philippi in northern Greece because of the hometown pride reflected when Luke mentions that city in Acts 16:12, and because of the hint that Luke was the man of Macedonia urging Paul to cross to Europe in Acts 16:9. If Luke was from Philippi in Macedonia, he would have been the only European or westerner writing in our New Testament, which explains why Luke's writings have a distinctive quality that appeals to those of us of the western world.

Luke was an eye-witness to much of the history of the early church. He introduces himself first at Troas in Acts 16:8-10 as a member of Paul's party, and was one of the few who remained with Paul to the

9

very end of the great Apostle's career at Rome (see II TIMOTHY 4:10-11).

Besides his own participation in many of the events in Acts, Luke had other material from which to draw. He had Paul's letters. He undoubtedly also had the personal reminiscences of Barnabas, Philip, Mark, Silas, Peter, and possibly Cornelius and other minor characters. More important, Luke had memories of extensive conversations with Paul. Perhaps Luke even had access to Paul's notes, diaries and written speeches, if there were such; Luke drew on all these sources and wrote Acts during Paul's last imprisonment in Rome, probably sometime between A.D. 60 and 65.

Why did Luke write Acts? The ostensible purpose was to instruct "Theophilus," an unknown inquirer about the gospel. Acts is Volume Two or a continuation of the account begun in the Gospel according to Luke, describing the spread of the Good News.

Some scholars think that Acts was written as a legal brief seeking Paul's acquittal, while others believe that Luke wrote to ease the tensions and unite the factions within the early church.

In any case, Luke was not writing a textbook on the history of the church. Although Acts is our only record of the period between A.D. 33 and A.D. 63 and the only history of Christianity written until Eusebius in A.D. 320, it is not a comprehensive account of the early days of the church. The Acts is actually a series of vignettes about the life of the early church, and there are many details which we wish Luke would have included.

Although Paul is prominently featured in Acts, Luke was not penning a biography of Paul. In fact, Luke stops abruptly before the end of Paul's life, leaving us in the air about his subsequent fate.

Volume Two of Luke's writings is usually called "The Acts of the Apostles." This is a very misleading title, since some Apostles are completely ignored and others, such as James, receive only passing mention. Still others, notably Peter and John, gradually recede to minor positions in Luke's account, while many who were not Apostles, such as Stephen, Philip, Barnabas and Silas, are leading characters in Acts.

Perhaps a more accurate title would be "The Acts of the Risen Jesus Christ by the Holy Spirit Through the Community of Believers." Starting with the Jewish seedbed, Luke shows us how the gospel spread through the Jewish community, then through outlying districts, then through the non-Jewish Middle East, then through

Gentile Asia, across to Europe and finally triumphantly into the great capital of the world—Rome!

Perhaps Luke originally planned to write a third volume in his series. Chapter twenty-eight seems to close on an incomplete note. On the other hand, perhaps Luke intended it that way. Possibly he wanted to have his reader, Theophilus, and others, including us, realize that the gospel must be spread yet farther. In this sense, The Acts of the Risen Jesus Christ by the Holy Spirit through the community of believers are still taking place.

Or, put it this way: You and I, today, are to read Acts only that we may write new chapters to the spread of the Good News from Galilee.

William P. Barker

Bower Hill Community Church,
United Presbyterian
Pittsburgh, Pa.

CONTENTS

Preface   9

1. INTERMISSION BETWEEN ACTS (ACTS 1)   17
2. GOD RE-INTRODUCES HIMSELF
    (ACTS 2:1-13)   23
3. THE EARLIEST FAMILY PORTRAIT
    (ACTS 2:14-47)   29
4. THE MAN BY THE GATE (ACTS 3:1-22)   33
5. A MATTER OF LOYALTY (ACTS 4:22)   39
6. THE TIE THAT BINDS (ACTS 4:23—5:11)   45
7. PROUD OF THE NAME (ACTS 5:12-42)   51
8. THE FIRST MANIFESTO AND THE
    FIRST MARTYR (ACTS 6 AND 7)   57
9. TRUMPETERS TO THE STRANGERS (ACTS 8)   65
10. SURPRISE AT DAMASCUS (ACTS 9:1-30)   73
11. THE DAY THE HORIZON STRETCHED
    (ACTS 9:31—11:18)   81
12. THE CITY OF "FIRSTS" (ACTS 11:19-30)   89
13. HOW CAN DICTATORS GET AWAY
    WITH MURDER? (ACTS 12)   95
14. "WE TURN TO THE GENTILES" (ACTS 13)   101
15. TALE OF FOUR CITIES (ACTS 14)   109
16. CONTROVERSY AND THE COUNCIL
    (ACTS 15:1-35)   115
17. "COME OVER TO MACEDONIA"
    (ACTS 15:36—16:12)   121

13

18. SINGING IN JAIL AT MIDNIGHT
  (ACTS 16:12-40)   127
19. THE NOT-SO-REASONABLE GOSPEL
  (ACTS 17)   133
20. "WE HAVE NEVER EVEN HEARD THAT
  THERE IS A HOLY SPIRIT"
  (ACTS 18:1—19:7)   141
21. RIOT AND FINAL FAREWELL
  (ACTS 19:8—20:38)   149
22. COURAGE BORN OF CONVICTION
  (ACTS 21:1—23:11)   157
23. "WHO DARES, WINS!" (ACT: 23:12—25:12)   165
24. VALEDICTORY IN CHAINS
  (ACTS 25:13—26:32)   171
25. "AND SO WE CAME TO ROME"
  (ACTS 27:1-44; 28:1-16)   177
26. THE NARRATIVE WHICH HAS NO
  ENDING (ACTS 28:17-31)   185

14

THEY STOOD BOLDLY

1

INTERMISSION BETWEEN ACTS

(ACTS 1)

IT WAS NOT A SPOOK STORY. IT WAS NOT A HALLUCINATION. IT WAS not a vision. Nor was it a myth. Jesus was alive!

The disciples were *certain* of the resurrection. They saw Jesus. They talked with Him, not just once, but repeatedly. They were so convinced that they were in fellowship with Jesus raised from the dead that they risked their necks to come out of hiding and return to Jerusalem. Even Jesus' brothers—once skeptical of His claims—were now among those who were convinced that He was alive again.

Unfortunately, however, the little group drew a faulty conclusion from the resurrection. To a man, they were positive that a divinely sent catastrophe would soon follow and the long-promised Kingdom would come. The disciples, obviously not having paid much attention to Jesus' teaching on this subject, had still not outgrown the Jew-in-the-street ideas of the Messiah and His Kingdom. They still clutched the old clichés, mouthed the old slogans about the Jewish state rising again and cowing every other nation into submission—silly, air-castle stuff that jingoistic politicians and revolutionary hotheads fed the street corner masses. Jesus had warned His followers against taking this heady blend of cheap religion and phony patriotism seriously, but the disciples had forgotten it.

"Lord, will you at this time restore the kingdom to Israel?" (ACTS 1:6) they kept asking. The form of the Greek verb here means that they pestered Jesus by asking Him the same question over and over.

The followers after the resurrection wanted a timetable as to when Jesus would do what they were so sure He would do: make Israel the top power in the world.

Jesus' answer was blunt: It was none of their business what God's secret plans were—there were certain matters that God had marked "Personal." Jesus once and for all quashed the inclination to fix dates, to pry into God's affairs, to want lurid details of the last days. Furthermore, He made it clear that it was not a timetable, but power, that the disciples needed.

The Kingdom would stretch around the world all right, Jesus made clear, but not at all as these followers expected. They were anticipating the wrong kind of act by God, thinking that God would intervene in such a way that they could merely sit by. Jesus promised, however, that what would happen next would happen through them.

The disciples were unprepared for any assignment. They were all set to be spectators of His ministry, not participants in it.

"You shall receive power," Jesus assured them, "when the Holy Spirit has come upon you; and you shall be my witnesses in Jerusalem and in all Judea and Samaria and to the end of the earth." (ACTS 1:8)

Here is the keynote of the Book of Acts. Here also is the charter of the church. The Greek word for "power" is *dynamis;* the disciples are to be a "dynamic" community, energized not by human power but by the Holy Spirit.

When this handful of believers is empowered by God Himself, Jesus tells them that they will accomplish extraordinary things. They will be witnesses in Jerusalem, Judea, Samaria, and in the farthest stretches of the world.

His witnesses in Jerusalem? Fantastic! Jerusalem was a hotbed of opposition, the very place where fanatical authorities had executed Jesus. Judea and Samaria? Preposterous! There were upwards of two million people throughout Palestine. What could a few dozen nobodies ever hope to accomplish for Jesus among so many? As far as witnessing elsewhere in the world, well, it was just too incredible to imagine. By all human standards, Jesus was commissioning them to do the impossible. How could this inept group of enthusiasts ever witness anywhere? They were, of course, reckoning without the promise of the Spirit.

Abruptly, Jesus was seen no more. The finale to His earthly ministry is called the ascension.

What happened exactly at the ascension? The account in Acts plays down the event. To the disappointment of some readers, Luke gives no breathtaking details. Our questions—"Is heaven 'up there' as a specific place?"; "How can a body suddenly become weightless or defy the laws of gravity?"—are out of place. The point is that Jesus was simply not seen anymore.

With Jesus gone, His followers floundered. Although they knew the facts of the cross and the resurrection, they drifted indecisively. "Jesus' earthly ministry is over," they seemed to say. *"Now* what?"

The last half of the first chapter of Acts is like the intermission between the acts of a play. There is an atmosphere of foot-shuffling and thumb-twiddling, of aimless milling in the corridors and waiting for something more to happen.

"Men of Galilee, why do you stand looking into heaven?" they were asked. (ACTS 1:11) The little band of believers stopped gawking at the sky and wandered back to Jerusalem. They went back to a familiar place, the Upper Room, a pathetic attempt to recapture the past when Jesus had been with them.

At least it must be said in their favor that they (a) prayed, and (b) stayed together. There was a gritty determination in their praying. The word in Greek, in fact, is the term used by an army besieging a walled citadel, hammering at the gates with desperate energy to break through and capture the city. Luke tells us that these early believers prayed with a dogged, we-will-not-give-up persistence.

When they prayed, they did not splinter into different groups, nor did they pray as isolated individualists, each in his own place and in his own way. They were together, physically together—an oft-overlooked fact. They also had a unanimity of purpose, a common concern that bound them together.

Nonetheless, before the coming of the Holy Spirit, something was lacking. Impetuous as always, Peter suggested they busy themselves with keeping the old organization going. Why not round out the ranks of the Twelve? There had been a vacancy since Judas' death. It struck everyone as a good idea to select a replacement.

There were two candidates: Joseph-Barsabbas (also known as Justus) and Matthias. Strangely, the disciples relied completely on chance in choosing one of these men. There is no mention of relying on the Holy Spirit. The two candidates simply drew lots, in the ancient Jewish manner, and Matthias won.

It is significant that the early church never again used this method to select its leaders. Neither Matthias nor Joseph-Barsabbas are ever mentioned again in the New Testament. It is tantalizing to imagine what became of Matthias, the man chosen to take Judas' place. Even more pathetic is the case of the man who almost became an apostle, Joseph-Barsabbas, the candidate who lost the toss.

All this lot-drawing was mere busy-work. The effort depended upon human ideas and human energies.

If the last mighty act of God had been the resurrection and ascension, today there would be no church. If the pattern outlined in the first chapter of Acts had continued, the apostles and others would never have left Jerusalem to witness. They would have formed a religious club, perhaps a "Jesus Memorial Society." Like other such groups, it would probably have had meetings, dues, minutes, and the usual club paraphernalia. In spite of valiant endeavors by loyal adherents to "keep the organization going", the band of believers in the Risen Jesus Christ would eventually have dwindled away and in time the memory of Jesus would have become an interesting footnote in the history books of the Middle East.

Their failure to understand God's purpose was all too human, and still familiar today. During the Vietnam crisis, an American soldier, knowing personally the horrors of savage fighting and the disgusting graft and incompetence of many Asian officials, and experiencing the frustration of existing in what seemed to him to be a stalemated war, blurted to a chaplain, "You don't suppose God is going to wind things up here soon, do you? With all the mess we're in, don't you think it's about time He did?"

All of us wonder, at times, "When is God going to do this or that?" Some even fish through the more lurid parts of later Old Testament prophecies or the Book of Revelation to get "secret codes" to clue us on God's schedule. Like the disciples after the resurrection, we accept the fact that Jesus rose from the dead, yet ask, "Yes, but what's next on God's agenda?"

Jesus makes it clear that we are not onlookers. Rather, we are called to participate in His ministry. He will not allow us to tug at His sleeve with our shrill little questions, "When, Lord?"

The question really is, "When are we going to wise up to what He has already done?" God has already acted. Through the life, death and resurrection of Jesus Christ, God has done everything for us that needs doing. Our responsibility is to be witnesses to what happened on the cross and through the Risen Lord.

Significantly, the word translated from the Greek for "witness" is exactly the same as our English word "martyr." In other words, a Christian witness is one who gives testimony by serving and suffering as well as speaking.

A few years ago in Thailand, a Fulbright scholarship was awarded to a bright Buddhist youngster from a remote, poverty-stricken village in north-eastern Thailand. Had it not been for the scholarship, this boy would have ended his education at the sixth grade and today would be probably tending water buffalo. He was sent to the Prince

Royal College, a Church-sponsored boys' school in Chiengmai, Thailand, and for the first time in his life, had enough to eat.

One night shortly after he arrived at the Prince Royal school, friends found him crying. They asked him why. He told them that it was because he had enough to eat while his family back home did not, and he felt bad because he had so much. His friends at the school, all Christians, passed the hat the next day and immediately sent a large sack of rice to the boy's family.

The boy was dumbfounded. How could these Christians care about his family? Why would they do anything for people whom they had never seen? What kind of strange persons were these Christians who were so concerned about him, a non-Christian? Why did they, who were also very poor, sacrifice their scant savings to send rice? Why would anyone "feel" his heartache, and why would anyone care enough about him, a penniless farmer's son?

He was so moved by the witness of the Christians at Prince Royal School that he wanted to learn more about them. Eventually, he decided that he would commit his life to Jesus Christ. Today, this brilliant scholar is the esteemed director of the Christian Student Center at Bangkok, and one of the dynamic younger leaders in the Thai Church.

Those Christians at Chiengmai, Thailand, knew the meaning of the word "witness."

Jesus makes clear that we are to be His witnesses not just across the street but across the world. All the trite clichés—"Charity begins at home," "Help our own first"—simply have no place in Jesus' scheme of things. There are no restrictions to God's care; neither can there be for ours. There is no "off limits" to His concern; neither dare we draw boundaries for compassion.

"You shall be witnesses in Jerusalem, Judea, Samaria and to the end of the earth," Jesus commanded. Had you and I been present that day, our reaction would have been, *"Jerusalem?* Wait a minute, Lord! They killed you there, remember? It's an uphill job to do anything there. *Judea?* Hold on! We'll have enough to keep us busy in Jerusalem. Let's not bite off more than we can chew. And did you say *Samaria?* Now Lord, you know that they are just not 'our type' up there. Besides, we'd be getting in over our heads. As far as witnessing at the ends of the earth, well, Lord, that is just plain impossible." We are so loud in our protests that we forget His promise: "You shall receive power when the Holy Spirit has come upon you."

Witnessing next door, next street, next town, next state, and "to the end of the earth" *is* impossible—if we have only ourselves to lean on. We must wait for the promised Spirit.

Sometimes it is necessary to do nothing *but* wait. In the British navy, whenever disaster strikes a ship, a signal called "the Still" is piped. Every man is trained to know that he is to stand stock still, do nothing but wait for orders. This prevents stupid, panic-driven acts and frantic, deadly haste.

With us in the church, there comes a time when we must wait for the Spirit and withstand the temptation to "get going" and "do something." In the post-war years in the church, we have been so preoccupied with "gearing for action" and "building up a program" that we have implied that the church is dependent upon our sweaty efforts and frenzied busywork.

Only the Holy Spirit, the promised Empowerer, will enable us to do the impossible. He only can give us what we need to be His witnesses. Our energy, our efforts will never be enough.

We may impress ourselves by our strenuous church-y activities. We may have entertaining preaching, well-oiled organization, souped-up program and a paid-for building. But we are playing church until we have been energized by the Holy Spirit.

God never goes back on His promises. The power of the Spirit is promised to those who wait for Him. Our task, if we have not yet been set aflame by the Holy Spirit, is to wait for the Pentecost needed by the church in every generation. Ask. Wait. He comes. But only to those who truly want Him.

22

2

GOD RE-INTRODUCES HIMSELF

(ACTS 2: 1-13)

THE DAY STARTED AS THE HEBREW HARVEST FESTIVAL. CALLED "Pentecost" because it falls fifty days after the beginning of the harvest, it was a holiday for the throngs in Jerusalem. No one dreamed that morning that the occasion would be remembered as the day of God's own harvest, the start of the church.

The ineffectual followers of the now-departed Jesus were in Jerusalem. Like hundreds of other Jews, they planned to participate in the ancient festivities. They still had no clear idea of how they could do much about carrying out Jesus' last instructions.

Suddenly, as unpredictably and inexplicably as a desert storm breaking on the Judean hills, He was with them! Mysterious and mighty, He was alive and near—nearer even than He had been when they had known Him in the person of the earthly Jesus.

Who was this dynamic invisible One? Who was this Energizer? The followers spoke of Him as the Holy Spirit, the Living God, the Risen Christ, or simply, "The Spirit." The same God who moved and worked through Jesus was—and is—moving and working still.

Though Jesus could not be seen or touched by His followers, His presence was as real to them as when they had sat at the table or walked along the road with Him, the Living Lord, except that now they had a stepped-up awareness of Him. God was re-introducing Himself to Jesus' followers.

Pentecost was not a pep rally. The coming of the Spirit was not merely enthusiasm the disciples fired themselves with, like a ball team charging out of the locker room. Some critics dismiss Pentecost as nothing more than morale which the disciples managed to work up from within themselves. The verb form in the Greek, however, is passive. The disciples' power was *given,* was *sent.* This power, Luke clearly states, was from a source outside themselves.

The surge of power and sense of His Presence which filled Jesus'

23

followers amazed some bystanders. Others thought the disciples were drunk. How else could anyone explain the excited state of what was normally a group of dour fishermen?

They were possessed, all right, Peter acknowledged, but they were not in their cups. Their exhilaration was not induced by alcohol—they were under the influence of the Spirit. If they seemed to be hilariously excited, it was simply an expression of sheer joy. God had fulfilled His promise, He had empowered them to do what He had commanded, and they could not contain their happiness.

The coming of the Spirit is *the* event in Acts. His empowering Presence that morning of Pentecost is the birthday of the Christian church.

The best way to understand Pentecost is to note its spectacular results. The coming of the Spirit enabled the disciples to preach so persuasively that three thousand people were convinced immediately. Jerusalem, that day, was filled with devout Jews from every province, of every language, dress, and culture, brought together because it was easier to travel in June. The list given by Luke includes those from the extreme East—Parthians, Medes; from the North—Armenia, Turkey, even present-day southern Russia; from the South—the African coast; the West—Rome. All of these heard and understood the mighty works of God. They immediately expressed their loyalty to Jesus Christ and committed themselves to be His group of followers —a highly risky thing to do.

At Pentecost, everyone understood what was being said. Although the original group of followers was fired up emotionally, it was not in a state of hysteria. These earliest Christians were enabled to communicate. Some scholars think that they were talking Galilean Aramaic—the commercial language of the Middle East at that time —which would have been understood by all even though everyone spoke a different dialect back home. In any case, regardless of origin, thousands of people received a first-hand knowledge of God's acts.

There was another dramatic gift of the Spirit to that group: a fellowship so deep and so meaningful that people were prepared and willing to sell their investments, pawn their possessions and part with their security. Just as pieces of metal cannot be joined except by the heat of a welder's torch, so these diverse individualists were united only by the power of the Spirit. It was not a voluntary association. They did not constitute themselves as another organization, or band together into a sort of club. Instead, they were fused by the Spirit into a fellowship so close with Jesus Christ and with one another that they would die rather than leave it.

We often sigh dreamily and say, "If only we could have been with them then." Many of our hymns feature an It-must-have-been-grand-back-then nostalgia. We look back with envy at Pentecost. We can see God in the past but not in our work week now. We can accept His being in history but not on our street today. "It's just that Jesus seems so long ago and far away," one woman stammered, explaining why prayer was so hard for her.

A young corporation executive was more blunt as he contended that Jesus lived so long ago that He was irrelevant to our society today. "What does Jesus know about cybernetics?" he demanded. "What does Jesus have to say about the corporate tax structure in the state of Pennsylvania?"

Breezily, a college student informed his parents that his dorm-mates and he had concluded after several midnight discussions that Jesus was a "back-number."

We can understand God at work nineteen hundred years ago. But what about now? True, God did act through a certain man at a certain time in a certain place. This Man was put to death on a cross and raised alive. The act was localized.

What happened in Palestine twenty centuries ago is made contemporary and universal by the Holy Spirit. He bridges the gap of years and spans the gulf of distance. The Holy Spirit makes Calvary and the Emmaus Road relevant to America, Europe, Africa, and Asia. He makes Jesus meaningful now. Because of the Spirit, Jesus is not a long-ago prophet tied down to an obscure corner of the Roman world. Because of the Spirit, Jesus' words spoken to men in A.D. 30 are unmistakably addressed to us. The Spirit re-presents Jesus to us.

Through the Spirit, God is constantly reaching out to us. He will not let us alone. He is continually opening and reopening the dialogue with us. Through the Spirit, God is still exerting every energy to transform us into new people, to mold us into a new community.

The Holy Spirit to those people at Pentecost was no vague power. The Spirit was always spoken of as "He," never as "it." He was not an impersonal "thing," not a mechanism, not a sort of supercharger to be switched on for an extra burst of power. The disciples' relationship to the Holy Spirit was a relationship with a Personal Being—the Empowerer, the Energizer, the Helper.

Never consider that the Holy Spirit is a sort of honorary immortality conferred upon Jesus by the disciples. Following the independence of the Philippines, General MacArthur was honored by the first congress with a citation which read, "His name shall be carried in

25

perpetuity on the company rolls of the units of the Philippine army, and at parade roll calls, when his name is called, the senior noncommissioned officer shall answer, 'Present in spirit.' "

Touching though such sentiment may be, the disciples were not paying tribute to Jesus by saying that He would be perpetually remembered as someone "present in spirit." Rather, they found that their lives had been invaded by Him who is the ever-present Spirit.

Through the Holy Spirit, we know that God is alive and at work now. The Spirit is God shifting Himself from the third person, "He," to the first person, "I." The Spirit uses the words of the Bible to communicate with us now, whenever we work seriously with the Scriptures. He re-presents Himself whenever we receive communion or observe a baptism. He fulfills Jesus' promises. He enables Jesus to speak everywhere today. He interprets the gospel to us. He convicts us. He helps us to be the people whom Jesus has called us to be. He renews us, a dying assemblage of weak, stubborn hypocrites, to be the church.

The Spirit offers us His gift of power to proclaim and witness. How can we ever put into language what Jesus Christ means? How can we get across to others that through Jesus, God has declared that He means to keep in contact with men, even to the point of bursting forth from a sepulchre? How can we convince others that He is so real and so near? As Martin Luther once put it, "When we speak about Jesus Christ, we are really babies talking brokenly in quarter-words." The Spirit fills in the missing words in our stammering efforts.

You say, "I cannot teach Sunday School; I have no training." He gives you the strength to handle a class. You say, "What good are my meagre talents in the choir?" He empowers you to help the church gather for worship. You say, "I'm afraid to speak up for what I know I should." He gives you the power to be a witness to the gospel in your club, your school, your office. You say, "I don't see how I can possibly bear up under such an impossible situation any longer." The Spirit gives you the stamina to keep holding on.

The Spirit brings us into communion together. He enables you to forgive me, me to forgive you, both of us to forgive our neighbor. He unites us separated people into His own family, the church.

A few years after World War II, two women came from Asia to visit American Presbyterian Churches and to witness to what Jesus Christ meant to them. One was Mrs. Uemura, the first woman to be permitted to leave Japan after the war. The other was Dr. Llano, a woman physician from the Philippines. They came to the States sepa-

26

rately and met for the first time one morning at breakfast. It was a painful encounter. When Dr. Llano saw Mrs. Uemura, all she could think of were the atrocities and devastation heaped on her family, her friends and her hospital by the Japanese invaders. Remembering the terrible suffering inflicted by the Japanese, Dr. Llano could not bring herself to say a word to Mrs. Uemura.

The following morning, Dr. Llano heard a knock at her door. Opening it, she was startled to find Mrs. Uemura. With bowed head, Mrs. Uemura quietly said, "Can you forgive me for what my people did to you and your people? Will you go to breakfast with me?"

Suddenly, they found themselves in each other's arms, crying. Then they sank to their knees side by side, hand in hand. Later, after they washed their faces, they went together to breakfast.

The Holy Spirit came upon them! He empowered them to do what they could not do themselves; He brought them together as the church. He still takes hold of believers—even today.

3

THE EARLIEST FAMILY PORTRAIT

(ACTS 2: 14-47)

A YEAR OR TWO AGO, A MAGAZINE ARTICLE STATED THAT ONE OUT OF four corporation executives is a Presbyterian. More than a few Presbyterians privately congratulated themselves that membership in their denomination was the badge of a successful executive. One dowager, pleased by the article, cooed to her fellow club-women, "Yes, most of the 'right people' are in our church."

Who were the *first* Christians? What were they like?

It is debatable whether they would feel comfortable in any Protestant congregation today. It is also open to question whether many respectable congregations today would want them or welcome them. The family portrait of the average Protestant congregation in the mid-twentieth century would be disturbing to the earliest believers.

Luke's portrait of the church shows that most at first still thought of themselves as Jews and as part of the synagogue tradition. They were not yet ready to welcome Gentiles, or quite prepared to forego the usual Jewish rites—especially circumcision.

Nevertheless, they were different. The earliest portrait of the Christian church shows distinctive family characteristics, some of which have lingered at least to some extent through successive generations.

The most obvious family trait among those early believers is that they were certain that a new age had dawned. Even without reading Peter's speech at Pentecost, it is obvious by his and others' actions that they were convinced that God had acted. A few days earlier, they had been operating furtively, meeting secretly, conversing guardedly. True, they knew that God had raised Jesus from the dead, but they were timid, hesitant men and women, hobbled by doubts and questions. Had it not been for the explosion of the new age at Pentecost, this group would have continued as a semi-clandestine group, meeting surreptitiously and believing privately.

No midnight knocks and secret passwords for those followers after Pentecost! They were suddenly on the streets in daylight. Their words, shouted to the world, had the authority and insistence of a mortar-barrage. Proof of the Holy Spirit's coming? Forget the academic theories and classroom philosophizing. Look at Peter and the others of the early church. Their actions bespoke the coming of God's new age.

Peter's words in the earliest sermon recorded in Christian history (ACTS 2:14-36) confirm this. He quoted the Old Testament prophet Joel, whose words had rung generations before in a Judah seemingly doomed by a devastating locus plague. Fast and repent, Joel had promised, and God would act in His own good time:

> And in the last days it shall be, God declares,
> that I will pour out my Spirit upon all flesh,
> and your sons and your daughters shall prophesy,
> and your young men shall see visions,
> and your old men shall dream dreams;
> yea, and on my menservants and my maidservants in those
> days
> I will pour out my Spirit; and they shall prophesy.
> And I will show wonders in the heaven above
> and signs on the earth beneath,
> blood, and fire, and vapor of smoke;
> the sun shall be turned into darkness
> and the moon into blood,
> before the day of the Lord comes,
> the great and manifest day.
> And it shall be that whoever calls on the name of the Lord shall
> be saved.

The quotation from Joel (ACTS 2:17-21) formed the backdrop for Peter's block-buster announcement—the long-promised New Age had come! God had, that very morning, fulfilled His promise. He had renewed his people by His great acts in Jesus Christ through the Holy Spirit.

Our world has heard of many "new ages" where power has been unleashed. One was on January 30,1933, in Germany, when a sometime-tramp-housepainter became chancellor and launched the Third Reich, which, he assured the world, was the start of a new age which "would last a thousand years." Another "new age," many trembling observers tell us, was launched on August 6, 1945, when the world's first atomic bomb was detonated over Hiroshima, obliterating nearly 80,000 human beings.

30

The New Age where God's great power—not man's—was let loose, began about A.D. 35 on the streets of Jerusalem. The New Age was no everything-will-be-rosy-now euphoria. The coming of the Spirit did not mean the end of human pain or problems; instead, it meant that men and women no longer faced these alone. No longer adrift or forgotten, they had the constant companionship of the ever-present Comforter. The New Age meant the certainty that God would complete His creation and was already doing so in their lives.

In the novel "Ulysses," the author, James Joyce, begins the book in the middle of a sentence. The book ends on the last page in the midst of the very sentence that starts the story back on page one, a literary device to emphasize Joyce's belief that life is, like the revolving links of a bicycle chain, an endless, senseless rotation of the same dreary components.

This is a viewpoint more generally accepted in our world than we like to admit. Listen to many of the popular songs, one index of our society's thinking. Or listen to the confession of a certain man working for a large company:

> I looked at the walls of my office this week. I suddenly realized that I had been looking at those same walls for twelve years. And I got to thinking. Twelve years ago, when I first looked at those walls, I told myself I would not be seeing them for long. I had myself moving into some of the carpeted sanctuaries behind certain key doors down the hall. Twelve years later, I am still in that same air-conditioned cubbyhole. I am stalled. By-passed. There will be twelve years more within those same walls. Sometimes when I think about it, it seems more like a sentence than a job. Twelve years: one sixth of my lifetime if I survive the average number of years of an American male. Or, if I count all the twenty-four years I will have spent boxed inside those walls, that will be one-third of my life. And I can't help but wonder—for what? All the lights that seemed to burn so brightly twelve years ago have winked out, one by one.

This sense of the futility and absurdity of life permeates not only our culture but nearly all of the world's religions. Man, they sigh, is trapped hopelessly in a cycle of meaningless existences and must try to escape through the oblivion of "nirvana," a state of "nothingness," or detachment and withdrawal from all human desire and involvement.

What happened to the earliest Christians in Jerusalem in A.D. 35

31

happens to anyone who asks God for a new beginning. The New Age dawns for anyone who accepts His pardon, His power, His presence.

The family portrait of the earliest believers shows another "family characteristic": a new understanding of Scripture. The Bible "spoke" to them. Previously, Peter and the others had fumblingly misread the Bible, had posed the wrong questions. Now, they understood that Jesus Christ was the "key" to Scripture and the Holy Spirit was His interpreter.

An African woman once was sitting outside her hut, tracing the letters of the words of her Bible with her fingers. It was obviously tedious work, and a bystander noticed her painful effort to work with Scripture. "Do you know," he asked her, "what you are reading?"

Her reply revealed a baptism by the Spirit and a wisdom from experience. "I am not reading this Book," she answered. "This Book is reading me!"

The Spirit unscrambles, clarifies, applies what seem to be mere words in the Bible so that they become God's Word to believers.

Luke's pen portrait of the first church shows that there was a strong sense of community among those touched by the Spirit. It was a new community, yet not exactly new because it was the fulfillment of what had been promised to the old community, Israel, for generations. Old Israel was turned inside out. No longer preoccupied with itself, Spirit-filled, the old community-made-new was now bursting with energy to announce God's New Age to the world.

The members of the Spirit-filled community prayed together, ate together, partook of the Lord's Supper together. They enjoyed one another's company. There was a contagious happiness about their gatherings, a genuine concern for one another and a sense of dependence upon one another. Those with means willingly shared with those of the community who were in need.

Suppose we were to write a one-page summary of what the church looks like today. What similarities to the early Jerusalem congregation could we note? What if we were to ask a non-church neighbor to write a description of what the church appears to be to him? How many "family characteristics" of the earliest believers would this neighbor observe in us? Some maintain the early characteristics of Christian believers have died out.

God still sends His Spirit. He still renews His church. Pray that He may send us His New Age!

4

THE MAN BY THE GATE

(ACTS 3:1-22)

THE CHURCH HAS ALWAYS HAD CRITICS. THROUGHOUT THE EARLY DAYS of the church there were detractors who sneered, "These enthusiasts for this dead rabbi, Jesus, are nothing but talkers. This 'power' they claim to have—how do we know they are not faking? Anyone can be carried away by emotions."

Emotionalism? Pretense? Only talk? Charges like these are serious —and cannot be refuted merely by hot denials.

Luke, astute medic that he was, knew that positive evidence to the contrary was the only answer to such criticisms. Doctor Luke had such evidence in his files: concrete examples of the power of the Spirit.

Luke recounts several fascinating medical case histories in Acts in which the Spirit operating through believers effects startling healings. The first and certainly one of the most dramatic happened shortly after the day of Pentecost. Peter and John, apparently still piously keeping to the old Jewish traditions, were on their way to the temple at three o'clock in the afternoon, when people were starting to move about the city again after the mid-day heat. As the two new Christians passed the Beautiful Gate above the Kidron Valley, they encountered a familiar procession—a hopeless cripple, being carried up to the gate by friends to take his usual station to beg hand-outs.

The first evidence that the Spirit had wrought some change in Peter and John is that they noticed the beggar. Although they had viewed him countless times, they had never really seen him before. "And Peter directed his gaze at him with John. . . ." (ACTS 3:4) Luke writes, emphasizing that these two Spirit-filled men riveted their entire attention on the unhappy cripple sprawled beside them, no longer casual observers of human suffering.

The Spirit gives men the power to see others as human beings instead of as bits of junk. The world is still the same world and its

33

people are still the same people. The Spirit, however, focuses our attention on those around us in need whom we have never noticed. As a near-sighted person fitted with glasses for the first time exclaims, "Why, I never saw the world like this before!" so the Spirit corrects our spiritual myopia so that we can see beyond ourselves. He allows us to "see" persons.

Luke shows that the early believers not only "saw" others, but reacted in astounding ways. Peter and John were more than talkers. Bold and provocative though their words were, they were nothing compared to what Peter and John did. Filled with the Spirit, they lifted the man to his feet and gave him the gift of the ability to walk!

Everyone was astonished. A moment before the beggar had been on his mat whimpering for a coin. Suddenly, he was standing before them, supported by feet that were no longer shrivelled claws. Such a startling event cried out for an explanation.

There was no blushing or false modesty with Peter and John, no mumbling, "Oh, it was really nothing." Instead their reaction was in effect, "Of course, he is walking, and it is astounding. But don't stare at us as if *we* did this." There was Another also present at the Gate Beautiful. He empowered them not only to make powerful speeches, but to make lame men walk. He was not the product of their emotions; He was the Presence of their Master.

Worship is hollow when we ignore others. We cannot go in to be blessed until we first care for those outside the door of the church. A helpless, crippled society lies before us, holding out its hand. If we, the church, have known anything of a Pentecost in our lives, we know also that we receive additional power only as we spend it in ministering to those who sit in hopelessness by the church door.

Filled with the Spirit, Peter, John, and the other early Christians seemed to be spilling over with power. The crippled beggar hoped for some of their spare change, but the disciples had slender worldly resources. "I have no silver and gold," Peter bluntly admitted, "but I give you what I have." And what Peter had was better than a Dun & Bradstreet rating or the power of a hefty bank account. "In the name of Jesus Christ of Nazareth," Peter commanded, "walk!" (ACTS 3:6) Peter, empowered by the name of Jesus Christ, did more than hand the beggar a donation—he allowed the Spirit to confer new life!

As the church, we can do more than offer handouts; we have more to offer than social service. We are given power to do more than

34

merely "something for charities." We have the power of the Holy Spirit! We are meant to lift a broken world to its feet.

A pastor of a congregation in the slums once told a group of solicitous suburban churchmen, "We don't want your food baskets at Christmas, or your old clothes and your cast-off toys. We don't want your offers to send paint to fix up our church basement. We want *you*. We need *you*. We would like to know that you care. That's what you can give us!"

We have tossed our extra nickels and dimes to those asking for help—then turned our backs and walked away. Important though money is (and even the slum pastor quoted above willingly concedes this point), it is more important that we offer ourselves as agents of the Spirit. He intends us to touch the shrivelled, dying community around us with the vitality given only by the Living Jesus Christ. Few of us, the church, have begun to realize the strength He offers us to heal the world.

Peter and John underlined the fact that it was Jesus Christ's strength, not theirs. ". . . Why do you stare at us," Peter demanded of the crowds, "as though by our own power or piety we had made him walk?" (ACTS 3:12) Peter unequivocably stated that Jesus Christ was the One empowering them to do such wonders. "*His* name," Peter insisted, "has made this man strong." (ACTS 3:16)

Never a man to pass up an opportunity to testify for Jesus, Peter began an extemporaneous speech in the temple courtyard.

"I care not for your prayers; let me see your praise," Robert Louis Stevenson once wrote. In Peter's impromptu address to bystanders after the miraculous healing, we see not pious posturing but the heartfelt praise of Jesus Christ that all the early believers felt.

The early church, from the very beginning, stood firmly on the fact of Jesus as God's unique and only complete revelation of Himself, crucified, raised alive, and present through the Holy Spirit. The lives of the first Christians unashamedly zeroed in on the *Person* of Jesus, not on "the religion of Jesus" or His "simple teachings." Trust in Jesus as God's Son and man's only Saviour was no odd doctrine rammed through by Paul and others at a later date. Peter's off-the-cuff sermon in the temple courtyard, Luke would have us know, was the accepted viewpoint of everyone in the early church. Jesus was the norm, the beginning, the end, the purpose, the vitality of the church, and without Him, there was simply no explanation for the church. The faith of those first Christians from the day of Pentecost rested squarely on the Person of the crucified, risen, living Jesus Christ.

"The God of Abraham and of Isaac and of Jacob, the God of our fathers, glorified his servant Jesus . . ." Peter stated (ACTS 3:13). The words in Greek for "his servant" can also be translated "his child" or, perhaps better, "his own Son." (The Greek word is *paidion,* the root for such English words as "pediatrics.") In other words, Peter was stating that Jesus had a unique relationship to the Father. The accepted idea then was that a son or child always was given the same personality as his parent, and Peter was saying, in effect, that Jesus had the same personality as God Himself. Jesus, to these earliest believers, was the One and Only complete revelation of God.

Peter added emphasis by referring to Jesus as "the Holy and Righteous One." (ACTS 3:14) These are no idle compliments. Again the Greek words are freighted with meaning. Jesus is the one pure and upright man, the only person who needs no correcting or improvement, the one individual who stands out as having a distinctly different relationship to God. Peter was trying to make clear that Jesus has been chosen and set apart by God and is exclusively God's.

And, touching on the central facts of Jesus' career, particularly His death, Peter continued that his Jerusalem listeners were responsible for killing "the Author of Life." (ACTS 3:15) Here is another Greek term that glistens with exciting suggestions. James Moffatt translates this as "the Pioneer of life." The New English Bible says it just as pithily: Jesus is He "who has led the way to life." Peter, with his penchant for blunt, picturesque workingman's words, said literally that Jesus is the "Trailblazer to Life."

Like a fisherman hauling up great lengths of net, each weighted with a rich catch, Peter brought up word after word describing Jesus, each heavy with meaning. Pointing to the ex-cripple, Peter dipped into the subject of Jesus as the Healer. "His name . . . has made this man strong whom you see and know;" Peter stated, adding, "Jesus . . . has given the man this perfect health. . . ." (ACTS 3:16)

Peter was touching on a topic close to the heart of Luke. Medical man Luke, who never ceased to be impressed with the Great Physician, deliberately uses the correct medical technical terms in Greek to emphasize that the one-time cripple's cure was no fluke or bit of flim-flammery. The formerly "hopeless case" was, through Jesus' power, now "sound," "firm," "solid," or "whole."

There had been the sign of the power of Jesus through the Holy Spirit at Pentecost. Here at the Gate Beautiful was proof of that same

power. Peter, Luke and those early Christians believed that through
the Holy Spirit, Jesus will ultimately complete His ministry of healing
so that the entire world is made whole. With insight into the universal
implications of Jesus' coming, Peter said, ". . . Jesus, whom heaven
must receive until the time for establishing all that God spoke by the
mouth of his holy prophets from of old." (ACTS 3:21) This word
"establishing", another term directly out of Luke's medical text-
books, means literally the "mending" of a broken bone or the "restor-
ing" of an injured part of the body. Peter and the early Christians,
Luke makes clear, saw Jesus as the God-sent Physician, who would
eventually bring complete healing to a broken, dying world.

With scarcely a pause for breath, Peter plunged on in his discourse.
Jesus is the Second Moses, an idea which must have shaken his
staunchly Jewish hearers to their sandals. Peter quoted Moses' words
in Deuteronomy 18:5-16: "Moses said, 'The Lord God will raise up
for you a prophet from your brethren as he raised me up.'" (ACTS
3:22) Peter insisted that Jesus is that promised prophet. Using
Moses' own words to support his point that Jesus is the new Moses,
Peter quoted Moses further: "'You shall listen to him (meaning
Jesus, Peter says) in whatever he tells you. And it shall be that every
soul that does not listen to that prophet shall be destroyed from the
people.'" (ACTS 3:23)

Did Peter remember the scene near Caesarea-Philippi months earlier when Jesus asked the disciples, "Who do men say that the Son of
man is?"? (MATTHEW 16:13) Did Peter recall the insistent way that
Jesus bored in: "But who do you say that I am?"? (MATTHEW 16:15)
Peter had only dimly understood who Jesus was at that time. His
impulsive answer, "You are the Christ, the Son of the living God,"
(MATTHEW 16:16) was more a reflex response than a carefully reasoned Christology. The experiences of the Transfigura-
tion, the Upper Room, Gethsemane, the courtyard of the High
Priest's house, Calvary, and the Emmaus Road followed. Peter's real
education in the school of Christ was brief, intensive, but productive.
At Pentecost, the Holy Spirit completed Peter's knowledge of who
Jesus was.

Sometimes a magnificent jewel will be polished and set in a mount-
ing. The jewel itself is not changed; it is only enhanced by successive
craftsmen. No one would claim that jewelers working on that precious stone changed its essential qualities or made it "more" a
diamond.

So, too, the essential priceless quality of the Christian faith was

37

given to the earliest believers at Pentecost. True, Paul and other thinkers such as the writer of "Hebrews" polished that diamond. True, the Council of Chalcedon in A.D. 451 mounted it permanently in its proper setting by making a complete and definitive declaration on the nature of the person of Jesus Christ (regarded as the orthodox Christological statement by the Eastern Orthodox, the Roman Catholic and most Protestant branches of the church). But the jewel in its basic form was already held by the church on that day when "there appeared to them tongues as of fire, distributed and resting on each one of them." Peter's sermon in the temple courtyard established this point once and for all.

Analogies are always dangerous. We have compared the church's understanding of Jesus Christ to a priceless diamond. We must be careful, however, that we do not push the image too far; we are too prone to regard the gospel as a lovely heirloom, a museum piece, an expensive ornament.

While it is true that the priceless wealth of the church through the centuries has been the news of Jesus Christ's life, death, resurrection and living Presence, this is no ancient, costly trinket. This is the A and the Z of our faith, the source and purpose of our lives.

Jesus Christ has been, is, and will be "the Holy and Righteous One" (ACTS 3:14), "the Author of Life" (ACTS 3:15). It is not enough to discuss what Peter and the first Christians believed—it is merely an exercise in history to comment on the early church's view of Jesus. The key question is still that one asked at Caesarea-Philippi: "Who do *you* say that I am?" (MATTHEW 16:15)

5

A MATTER OF LOYALTY

(ACTS 4: 22)

IT DID NOT TAKE LONG FOR WORD OF PETER'S SOAPBOX SERMON TO reach the authorities. Huffing with indignation, they swarmed down to the courtyard. They needed to hear only a few sentences of Peter's discourse to turn them livid with fury. The offending words? Peter's claim that Jesus was raised from the dead.

"That iconoclast from Galilee again!" the temple authorities exploded. They had had an unpleasant spring because of Jesus. The troublemaker had brazenly set Himself over them and all that they stood for. Engineering Jesus' "removal" had not been easy: Pilate had been his usual difficult self. Then there had been the report of the tomb broken open and the corpse missing. Even fat bribes to the guards to spread the lie that the body had been stolen had not squelched the whispering that Jesus was alive. Obnoxious, persistent rumors kept flicking through Jerusalem that He was still meeting with His followers in some upper room, on the road to Emmaeus, in Galilee. And now the brash invasion of the sacred temple grounds with these preposterous ideas! And by a couple of common Galilean fishermen!

Lock them up! Bread and water and a night on a stone floor sober any enthusiast. This wild talk had to be stopped. It could wreck everything that the temple stood for.

The next morning, all of the temple power structure turned out for the hearing. They were expecting to find two chastened countrymen. A night in detention and the awesome dignity of the High Priest's gathering always left rural problem-makers whimpering for pity. Instead, the Jerusalem aristocrats were amazed by Peter's and John's eloquence and zeal.

The authorities maintained a supercilious tone, demanding, "By what power or by what name did you (with the 'you' sneeringly implying 'men like you') do this?" They tried to badger Peter and

John by asking them repeatedly: Who gave such people as you the authority to carry on like this? (The form of the verb in the Greek means that they kept asking the question over and over).

The collision of Peter and John with the temple authorities was the first of a long, often bloody, history of conflict for the church. The staggering number of arrests of Christians in Acts makes the record read like a police blotter. Contrary to the docile, at-home-here coziness of the church in today's society, the earliest church was an irritant. The first Christians upset things; they disturbed people.

When the church has been most filled with the Holy Spirit, it has been most uncomfortable in the world. Society is edgy toward people who take the gospel seriously. Whenever the Spirit introduces the living Jesus Christ to a group, He inevitably causes that group to listen to a different voice, to march to a different cadence. The world resents the threat posed by anyone who puts Another ahead of it.

The first arena of conflict was with popular religion. Peter and John found themselves out of step with the prevalent pattern of belief. They were in a tight spot—they knew that the same authorities glaring at them had successfully contrived to crucify Jesus, and that the church was young and frail. Perhaps the thought crossed their minds to play down the differences that Jesus made, to placate the authorities. Peter, after all, had used oily words to try to allay the suspicions of a servant girl in the courtyard of the High Priest's house on the night of Jesus' arrest.

Not this time. Luke says simply that Peter was "filled with the Holy Spirit." (ACTS 4:8) The Spirit would not let Peter be accommodating to the temple officials by minimizing Jesus. In fact, Peter unequivocally stated that the crippled beggar was healed by none other than Jesus, adding in the next breath, "whom you crucified." (ACTS 4:10) Peter did not sidestep the key point of faith, nor ease up on his audience for politeness' sake.

What a contrast to the oft-heard plea, "Let's not be sticky about Christianity. After all, all religions boil down to the same thing. Let's cut out obnoxious creeds and the rubbish of dogmas. Let's get back to the ethical values and basic philosophy of every religion."

In February, 1959, at the South Pole, seventeen men in the operation "Deep Freeze IV" in their spare time built a sixteen-foot-square chapel. Called the "Chapel of Our Faith," the structure contained an altar over which hung a picture of Jesus, a crucifix, a star of David, and a lotus leaf symbolizing Buddhism. An inscription on the wall read, "Now it can truly be said that the earth turns on a point of faith."

Hearing of the South Pole "Chapel of Our Faith," one enthusiastic layman called on his minister and boomed, "That's what we should be doing here!"

An "all-faiths" altar was dedicated at the University Interreligious Center of a large eastern university. The altar was skillfully engineered so that it would revolve, exposing any one of four sides, one for Protestant services, another for Roman Catholic masses, a third for Jewish worship. The fourth side was flipped to the front for programs sponsored by "other faiths."

All reports indicate that this reflects the thinking of the current college generation. "All religions lead to God. Christianity joins with other faiths in a common search for truth," wrote one student to her pastor.

It would have been expedient for Peter and John to have mumbled some platitudes about "religion" that morning at the hearing before the High Priest and his henchmen. They might have won smiles of approval with a few complimentary statements about the way the High Priest and the authorities helped add to everyone's insights on "faith" and enabled people in Jerusalem to climb a little higher in their search for truth. Peter and John might have spread their hands disarmingly and said, "Now Jesus was really not so different from others. Basically, He was saying the same thing." The earliest churchmen might have won immediate acquittal by a reasonable, broadminded down-grading of Jesus Christ.

Instead, fired by the Spirit, Peter gave a ringing testimony to the uniqueness of Jesus. ". . . There is salvation in no one else," Peter cried, "for there is no other name under heaven given among men by which we must be saved." (ACTS 4:12)

The early Christians spoke no idle words about Jesus' adding to man's quest for "spiritual values" or Jesus' being an interesting variation of great religious teacher. Jesus was the stone ". . . which has become the head of the corner." (ACTS 4:11) Peter and John were uncompromising on the place of Jesus Christ. His name, they insisted, is the only name that saves men.

Biblical scholars keep finding evidence of this as they try to translate the Scriptures into foreign tongues. For example, there is no word for "care" in the Thai language. One translator comments, "The name of Jesus Christ puts this word into our vocabularies." No name in Thai, or any "other name under heaven," can convey the Father's saving care except that of Jesus Christ.

Jesus Christ *saves!* The early church knew this. The Spirit empowered these people to testify to this fact. The very title "Saviour" was

41

chosen deliberately. Ordinarily, the term "Saviour" was reserved exclusively for emperors and royalty. Only one private individual—the Greek philosopher, Epicurus—was ever called *soter* or "saviour," and even Epicurus was given the title as an accolade. None of these "saviours," however, could truly save anyone. The title, the church knew, fitted only One. As men and women who knew the disintegration of life before He became the cornerstone for their existence, they could only shout, "There is salvation in no one else!" (ACTS 4:12) This was no party-line doctrine; this was their personal life's experience.

Predictably, the temple authorities did not take well to Peter's words. The hearing was not proceeding at all along the usual lines. The two bold fishermen standing in front of them were not members of the nation's power structure. They were peasants—unpolished bumpkins, untutored commoners, with neither standing or education. It was galling to discover that two such men had grabbed the initiative, making it seem that the High Priest and officialdom were the ones on trial. Who were these two Galileans?

The Jerusalem bluebloods and V.I.P.'s were even more uncomfortable when they recognized that Peter and John had been with Jesus. Perhaps their consciences told them how guilty they had been in condemning Jesus. Guilt can do strange things. Although reason told them that the lame beggar was most certainly healed, their guilt would not allow them to acknowledge Jesus as the source of the cure. Angry and frustrated, they dismissed Peter and John and conferred in private. They were cornered and they knew it. The only way out was to issue threats.

Calling in Peter and John again, the Council of the High Priest and the temple leaders solemnly warned the two disciples not to ". . . speak or teach at all in the name of Jesus." (ACTS 4:18)

Spirit-filled men are not easily intimidated. Peter and John were not moved by the bluster and pressure, retorting, "Whether it is right in the sight of God to listen to you rather than to God, you must judge; for we cannot but speak of what we have seen and heard." (ACTS 4:19-20)

Peter and John walked out free men—temporarily. Although they won an acquittal this time, the battle was not concluded. It was only a lull while the authorities plotted sterner methods to silence those speaking and healing in the name of Jesus.

Christians will always be in conflict with the status quo. Society constantly says to the church: "Go along with us. We know what is good and what is bad. Let us be the arbiter." Culture tries to rule as God. Society attempts to impose its will. There is always the unspoken threat: Do as we say—or else.

Christians from the very earliest days have been pressured to knuckle under. Peter and John were harassed in several ways. They were called names; the terms "uneducated, common men" (ACTS 4:13) were meant as insults. In addition to personal slights, Peter and John were subtly slandered by the innuendo that they were disobedient to the law and disloyal to their leaders. Peter felt called upon to refute these vague charges by answering, "Whether it is right in the sight of God to listen to you rather than to God you must judge." When the more genteel forms of intimidation failed to put Peter and John in their places, the authorities resorted to open threats. Succeeding chapters of Acts show that the first century society, whether in Judea, Asia, or Rome, was prepared to take whatever steps necessary to carry out those threats.

It was no accident that early Christians were called *atheoi* or atheists. Those believers in Jesus were non-believers in what the world thought sacred. They repudiated the popular gods; they slighted society's creeds.

"Be a tool to achieve our goals," society also tells the church. "Help us to preserve our American way of life."

Pleasant though our American way of life is, evil though Marxism is, the main, number-one purpose of the church is not to bolster America or defeat communism. The mission of the church is not to carry in the gospel to shore up anything.

To those who want to make the church simply one more antidote against communism, divorce, or juvenile delinquency, and to those who try to enlist the church as one more booster of a "good cause," we must answer, "We will not be used, we dare not be used by anyone except the Holy Spirit."

Behind all the smiles and "suggestions" by society to the church to "Go along with us," there is always an unspoken "—Or else!" That "—Or else!" is being felt more and more in these times. "Adopt our ideas on race and housing," the public insists. "After all 'those others' are really not 'our type,' and 'they' would be happier in their 'own church' or their 'own neighborhood.' Isn't 'our church' for people like us?" More than a few Spirit-filled Christians today have defied the dictates of society and paid the cost in lost friendships or even lost jobs.

How were Peter, John, and the other early Christians able to stand up under such pressure? How can we? We ask ourselves, ". . . By what power or by what name did you do this?" (ACTS 4:7)

"Then Peter, *filled* with the Holy Spirit . . ." Luke tells us (ACTS 4:8), meaning that the Holy Spirit took possession of Peter's mind, saturating him completely.

When any believers allow Him to take possession of their lives, He promises, He confers upon them the power and the name to face anything.

6

THE TIE THAT BINDS

(ACTS 4: 23–5: 11)

THE ONLY U.S. REGIMENT IN BURMA DURING WORLD WAR II WAS AN outfit known officially as the 5,307th Composite Unit (Provisional). Alone, cut off, operating behind Japanese lines in the steamy jungles, the men in three disease-decimated battalions of the unit fought for months without recognition or advancement. Although the survivors were later dubbed "Merrill's Marauders" by a newsman, at the time of their exploits they thought of themselves only as a forgotten handful carrying on against impossible odds. One night, as a squad lay in the rain for hours without supper, pinned down by sniper fire, one nameless G.I. was overheard mumbling to no one in particular, "Where are the 5,306 *other* composite units?"

Infantrymen and Christians have much in common in this respect. Both need the support of others. Both feel the loneliness of facing heavy opposition. Both sometimes think that they are cut off. Church leaders, like military men, sometimes forget the need to help the man out on the front lines to know that he is not isolated or forgotten but is backed by a powerful unit.

The members of the early church stood by one another, knowing a closeness, a camaderie which bolstered those having to make a lonely stand. Without idealizing them (for they were very human on occasion, as we shall note), we recognize that they felt a responsibility for one another. There was a genuine community among them.

Luke reiterates this point throughout the early chapters of Acts. In the interlude between Peter's first and second arrest in the temple precincts, for example, Luke tells how the Apostles were supported by other members of the Christian community.

"When they were released, they went to their friends," (ACTS 4:23) Luke reports of Peter and John. They did not wander back, lonely and dispirited, to carry on their missionary tasks disconnected from other believers. Instead, like a patrol returning to a crack unit

45

from a dangerous mission, Peter and John signed in immediately with the others. There was a solidarity among the earliest believers, each realizing how much the others depended on him, and how much he depended on them.

How did they fortify each other? What did they do to support one another?

Luke tells that these first believers prayed. And what praying it was! It was not the namby-pamby stuff that tries to pass as prayer in the church in our time. To begin with, ". . . they lifted their voices *together* to God. . . ." (ACTS 4:24) They were not loners, absorbed only in their private needs. Prayer was not the refined form of selfishness it sometimes is for church people today. Prayer was work *by* the entire community of believers *for* the entire community of believers.

Luke allows us to eavesdrop at the impromptu prayer meeting held immediately after Peter's and John's release. There was nothing casual about the prayers of this gathering. "And when they had prayed," Luke says, "the place in which they were gathered together was shaken. . . ." (ACTS 4:31)

Church-shaking praying! Contrast this to the weariness and dreariness of most Protestant worship today.

Their "secret"? Like a refrain, Luke's words—". . . and they were all filled with the Holy Spirit. . . ." (ACTS 4:31)—keep recurring in the text of Acts.

The Holy Spirit made God real. These believers were praying to a "Sovereign Lord" (ACTS 4:24), not to an Absentee Designer.

In some circles, it is "in" to speak of the "death of God," meaning that He is something like a retired chairman of the board, no longer involved but merely an honorary head of the operation. The Spirit stabs us awake to the awareness that God has definitely not stepped out of the picture. No "Grand Old Man," God is alive here, not "off in heaven." Through the Spirit, He makes it clear that He is still the main One who acts.

The Spirit interpreted God. The earliest Christians were led to pray to the God who deliberately chose to get His hands dirty—even bloody. The Spirit led them in a dialogue with One who had been at work in the world in the past and insisted on being involved in human affairs in the present.

Through the Holy Spirit, the first believers were able to make sense out of history. In their prayers, they show that they believed God had even successfully out-maneuvered "Herod and Pontius Pilate with the Gentiles and the peoples of Israel" (ACTS 4:27) at the cross. Their combined hellishness had not boxed in God. God, these Christians

46

knew, had thwarted the majority, had upset the schemes of the power clique—*and could do it again anytime!*

God is at work in His world. He is still sovereign. He—not death, not dictators, not evil, not despair—is in complete charge. "While thou stretchest out thy hand to heal," prayed the group of disciples, recognizing that God is unceasingly and tirelessly exerting Himself to bring about His new creation.

Just as the earliest members of the family of believers bolstered one another by their prayers, the church still strengthens its members through intercessory prayer.

A flier, shot down in the Pacific, was forced to spend many uncomfortable days on a raft before being picked up. Not a particularly strong Christian until the time on the raft, he wrote back to his parents after his rescue:

> What kept me going during those days was knowing that you folks and everybody over at the church would be praying for me. I remember how you used to pray at supper for various people, Dad, and I knew you'd be remembering me. I also remember how we'd always pray for the sick and the guys in the service and others on Sundays at church, but it never meant much to me. Until this past week. It's funny, but you know those prayers meant everything while I was sitting on that raft.

A missionary, isolated and sometimes discouraged after years of thankless service in a remote jungle, wrote back, "It has been an awful day, but I'm not down in the dumps. Somebody back home must have been praying for me again today."

Our prayer for others may be an invisible means of supporting them, but it nonetheless does more than we usually understand.

Members of the early church also gave more visible means of support to one another. As need arose, those with money or property shared. Through the Holy Spirit, they had a sense of responsibility toward each other, even parting with their possessions to help one another.

A sure sign of whether or not a conversion is genuine is if a man's pocketbook has been affected.

When Frankish tribes were first reached by Christian missionaries, many of the wild chieftains and their followers were baptized en masse. Frequently, however, as these warriors waded into the river to be immersed, they would hold their right hands and their battle-axes carefully above their heads, high above the water. The tribesmen

47

then went on pillaging and battling as before, claiming that their fighting arms and weapons had never been baptized.

We sometimes take the blessings of the gospel so much for granted that we feel little compulsion to give our money, but the more we receive of God's goodness, the more we should want to give.

Visitors at McKean Leprosy Hospital in Thailand are always surprised. Although over 95 percent of the Thai people—including entering patients—are non-Christians, McKean exists because of Jesus Christ. New patients quickly realize that the medicines and care offered them are because of Him. Incredibly grateful for the Christian community at McKean (where all the staff but two are Christians with arrested cases of leprosy) almost eighty percent of the patients eventually profess their faith in Jesus Christ and are baptized. Most astounding, although these Christian lepers subsist on a tiny income from handcrafts and a miniscule government dole, every one of them in the McKean Church is a tither! The only explanation is that one gives in proportion to one's gratitude.

Spirit-touched people have a reckless, hilarious quality about sharing their possessions. ". . . No one said that any of the things that he possessed was his own. . . ." (ACTS 4:32) they said in the earliest congregation. Their possessions already belonged to Jesus Christ; hence, these first Christians were simply trustees for what was actually Jesus' property. Led by the Spirit, they knew that they saw Jesus in the eyes of any hungry, chilly, sick, or helpless brother or sister. Their money, land and investments had to be used to feed, to clothe, to heal others in the family of believers.

Typical of the group was Joseph, a Levite of a distinguished Cyprus family, who spontaneously sold a piece of land and turned over the proceeds to the church leaders to help others. There was no fanfare; there was no bronze tablet. The best reward this Cypriot Levite received was the nickname "Son of encouragement" or Barnabas.

Tragically, not all were sons of encouragement. Luke recounts an incident which tore the unity of the early congregation in Jerusalem.

Ananias and Sapphira were members of the Christian family. In contrast to Barnabas, they schemed to appear to be generous, but at the same time, they secretly kept part of what they pretended to give.

Ananias' and Sapphira's sin was not so much hoarding as breaking down community trust. They lied. This act of deceit toward God and others undermined the unity of the early church. Peter tried desper-

48

ately to repair the damage by going directly to the two hypocrites. He was honest with Ananias and laid it on the line: Ananias had cheated not just his fellow church members, but God. Peter did not evade the issue, did not try to be "nice," did not pretend that there was only a little "misunderstanding."

Peter and other early believers regarded their fellowship in the church as something so sacred to them that they could be completely honest with each other. Aware of God's care toward a wayward brother, they knew that they had to go to that brother themselves.

Luke in his first volume had quoted Jesus' words on this subject: "Take heed to yourselves; if your brother sins, rebuke him, and if he repents, forgive him." (LUKE 17:3) The earliest churchmen took Jesus' instructions literally. These Christians did not sidestep a sticky situation; they realized that they were meant to strengthen the unity of the church by going to one another to correct, encourage, and admonish—yet always in love.

In the episode described by Luke in ACTS 5:1-11, the effect was dramatic. "When Ananias heard these words, he fell down and died. . . ." (ACTS 5:5). Although Luke gives us no clinical details, it is safe to assume that Ananias dropped over from the sheer shock of being confronted by representatives of the community he had hurt. Three hours later, when Sapphira was exposed as an accomplice in deceit and was informed of her husband's sudden demise, she, too, collapsed and died.

In reading the account of Ananias and Sapphira's startling fate, we are shocked by what seems to be a harshness on the part of Peter and the other church leaders. Although the sudden deaths of Ananias and Sapphira had a sobering effect on everybody, Luke did not record the facts to scare people into line. The important thing to note is the openness, the honesty, and the responsibility among the members of that first congregation. Throughout the infancy of the church, in spite of squabbles and selfishness, they sensed an obligation of deep concern for one another. Peter's motives in going to Ananias and Sapphira were the best—he cared enough about this pair of hypocrites to be honest with them.

St. Augustine's is an Episcopal parish in the heart of the notorious "Hell's Kitchen" area of New York City, where, under the creative leadership of an unusual team of clergy and social workers, a meaningful parish program has been developed. In spite of the variety of racial and ethnic groups, the Holy Spirit has knit them into a fellowship of mutual concern that has expressed itself in unusual ways. On the walls of the St. Augustine hall are inscribed words that should be

49

emblazoned on every church building in the world: THE STORY OF EVERY PARISH SHOULD BE A LOVE STORY.

In verse eleven of the fifth chapter of Acts, Luke slips in a word which he has not previously used. It is the Greek word *ekklesia* (root of our English word "ecclesiastic"), translated as "church," a word dripping with meaning in Greek. Literally, the word for "church" means "called out" or "called together." In Greek, for example, the word was used to describe how the citizens of a city would be summoned or "called out" when threatened by an invasion or emergency.

There are many overtones in this word for "the church." It suggests that we are draftees rather than volunteers in God's service. God has summoned us. "You did not chose me," Jesus reminded His followers (including us), "but I chose you. . . ." (JOHN 15:16)

The church is not a club or lodge that we decide to "join" and support. We are not free to withdraw or resign or retire when it does not "meet our needs," or when things are not going the way we like.

Although today we sometimes forget that the church is more than a random collection of individual believers, there is a corporate dimension, a community aspect to the church that the first Christians took very seriously. We are "called *together*." We do not fight informally in our own little wars against evil as the whim strikes us any more than we fought private little wars as individualists against the Axis in 1939-45.

To those earliest believers, "the church" was not a building somewhere in Jerusalem. Nor was it the Apostles and so-called "important" people. Nor was it the organization or structure. The church was the community of those called together by the Holy Spirit to continue the ministry begun through Jesus Christ's life, death, and resurrection.

Because they were "together" because of God's act and God's call, they stood by one another, sustained one another, corrected one another. Because they knew that God would not let them go, they could not let go of one another.

We sometimes get on one another's nerves in the church—we fail each other, we hurt one another, we all behave as hypocrites. Sometimes, we are ready to "quit the church."

God has not quit on us. Because He has not turned His back on us, neither can we leave one another as the church. He means for us to be together; He intends to have us stay together.

50

PROUD OF THE NAME

(ACTS 5: 12-42)

A CERTAIN FOUR-YEAR-OLD, HOME AFTER A SUNDAY SCHOOL LESSON about Jesus' disciples, was asked what she had learned that morning. The youngster lisped, "I learned about Jesus' samples."

After Pentecost, the disciples *were* samples of Jesus. Remembering that Jesus had sent them to continue His work, they dubbed those who had known him "Apostles," meaning "ones who are *sent.*" They were given His presence and His power, and they presented the authorities with daily samples of this power and presence in action, right on the temple steps.

The results were spectacular. Great numbers became believers, ". . . multitudes of both men and women. . . ." (ACTS 5:14) More astonishing, great numbers were healed. Ill people were brought from Jerusalem, even carried in from the surrounding villages and countryside. The very shadows of the Apostles were believed to have healing properties.

We would call these cures "miracles." To Luke and the other early Christians, however, these healings were simply "signs and wonders." In contrast to many faith-healers today who keep one eye cocked on the TV camera and the other on the collection plate, these "samples" of Jesus refused to take any credit for themselves. They shrank from publicity. Although they could have played up the sensational side of these healings and used their cures as a "come-on," they shunned the temptation. They would not exploit others or capitalize on their gifts to heal. The healings were "signs"—signs of the power of the Holy Spirit. Too, they were "wonders," the inexplicable workings of the Spirit. The disciples were grateful for these "wonders," but they made certain that all of them were attributed to the Holy Spirit, not to themselves. He was the Source. Peter, John, and the others were merely conductors, not the cause, of that Power.

These Spirit-filled disciples were no innocuous do-gooders as far as

The Establishment in Jerusalem was concerned. Jesus had been such a threat to these rulers that they had resorted to a cross to get Him removed. The disciples' activities were samples of the same trouble which Jesus had caused in the temple.

The nation's decision-makers, realizing the threat which Jesus' followers posed, said to each other, in effect, "A night in detention and a stiff warning were not enough for these agitators? All right; this time, we'll show them! We'll convince them that we mean business. They can't fool around with us! These peasant preachers need to be taught a lesson. We've got to put them in their place. The very idea—taking over the temple with their crazy talk and filling the courtyard with a rabble of groaning invalids!"

This time, they put Peter and John in the public jail. "The common prison" (ACTS 5:18), described by Luke as the place of the Apostles' incarceration was a well-guarded stone cell, not the place of detention in which Peter and John were detained overnight during their first brush with the temple bigwigs described in ACTS 4:3.

It is fascinating to conjecture how the Apostles got out of the Jerusalem prison that night. Their story might be one of the classics of "Great Escape" literature. Some suggest that there might have been a Christian among the guards whose identity was kept carefully hushed for security reasons. Others have intimated that perhaps there was a sympathetic jailor who, realizing the innocence of the Apostles, quietly turned the locks in the middle of the night.

There was inside help, all right, Luke emphasizes, but it was not a clandestine human agent whose name was never revealed. Luke distinctly points out that the Apostles' release was God's doing. The identity of the "messenger" or "angel" was unimportant.

"Go and stand in the temple," the Lord's spokesman commanded, "and speak to the people all the words of this Life." (ACTS 5:20)

Back to the temple? The disciples must have shuddered—that was sticking their heads in the lion's mouth. "Why not a rest, a break for a time?" they must have thought. "Wouldn't it be better to keep quiet for a time, let things simmer down? Or, couldn't we testify in some 'safe' place? We'll just get clapped into irons again—or worse—if we go back to the temple!"

God never releases a man from a tight spot for that man to have an easy time of it: He has bigger plans in mind for that person. This was true with the Apostles' release from the Jerusalem jail. There was a purpose behind that deliverance: to have them go right back to the temple and continue their testimony for the Risen Jesus Christ.

Although sympathetic to the Reformation in Paris in 1533, John Calvin was more anxious to be a secluded scholar than a Reformer. After Calvin's friend, Nicholas Cop, preached a sermon which Calvin had had a hand in writing, the authorities tried to seize both men for heresy. John Calvin, disguised as a workman, fled from the city on foot just in time to escape arrest, hoping to settle down quietly and safely with his books and continue his studies. A few months later he wrote, "When I promised myself an easy, tranquil life, what I least expected was at hand." Detouring through Geneva where he had planned only to stay overnight while enroute to Strassburg, Calvin was pushed into being involved in turbulent Geneva's reformation. God's "angel" or messenger on that occasion was fiery William Farel, upon whose insistent command Calvin reluctantly stayed in Geneva. He later said, "I felt as if God from heaven had laid His mighty hand upon me to stop me in my course . . . and I was so stricken with terror that I did not continue my journey."

Much as the Apostles might have longed to escape the dust and danger and loll at ease in the shade, they knew the Lord's command. And back to the temple they went.

Early the next morning they were teaching in their usual places. The scene almost has an air of comedy about it. At the same time the disciples were holding forth, the High Priest and his party were gathering for the formal hearing, assuming, of course, that Peter and John were still locked up. It is amusing to imagine the consternation when guards, chief priests, and the temple officialdom discovered that the Apostles were not only missing from their cells but were at that very moment preaching outside on the temple steps!

There was no humor, however, among the members of the Council and Senate of Israel when the Apostles were marched before that assembly shortly afterward. As voiced by the High Priest, there were two charges against the Apostles. The first and only specific charge was that the disciples had disobeyed the order not to preach. The second accusation, fuzzier but no less serious, was that the Jesus' followers were verging on sedition. The authorities, nettled because they were being tagged with the blame for the crucifixion of Jesus, took the disciples' words as an affront to their authority.

Peter's words did nothing to salve the power structure. "We must obey God rather than men," he affirmed. (ACTS 5:29) Hammering insistently on the theme which irked the authorities, Peter as spokesman for the Apostles continued, "The God of our fathers raised Jesus whom you killed by hanging him on a tree." (ACTS 5:30)

53

Peter effectively answered the two charges. By his insistence that obedience was due first to God, he disposed of the accusation that the Apostles were disobeying the authorities.

The second charge, with vague innuendoes that they were being disloyal to the heritage of Israel, was harder to refute. Speaking for all the early Christians, Peter deliberately used the words, "The God of our fathers," pointedly associating the church with the history of Israel. Neither Peter nor the other earliest churchmen would sever themselves from the people with whom God had covenanted through Abraham, Moses, and the prophets. They could not imagine themselves as anything but a continuation of the covenanted community. Peter's words show unmistakably that the early church consciously thought of itself as in the stream of the Old Testament.

The same God who acted in the history of Israel, Peter declared, has raised Jesus from the dead and exalts Him "at his right hand as Leader and Savior." (ACTS 5:31) Strong words, these! God has sent Jesus ". . . to give repentance to Israel and forgiveness of sins." (ACTS 5:31) The raising of Jesus Christ, the disciples make clear, is a turning point, a new beginning for the nation. The resurrection, Peter is saying, must be recognized by everyone—including the High Priest's party—as the key event in all of Israel's history.

Old fisherman Peter had his own personal word for Jesus. The translators blandly put it into English as "Leader" (ACTS 5:31). The word in Greek is *archegos,* a seaman's term. In Peter's day, many ships had a crew member who was an unusually strong swimmer. If anything happened to the ship, this crewman would tie a rope around his waist, dive overboard and swim to shore. After attaching the rope on shore, he would assist others who were making their way to safety by clinging to the line. His name was the *archegos.*

Peter thought of Jesus as The Archegos in life. In fact, Peter used the term in both of his appearances before the Council at Jerusalem (ACTS 3:15 and ACTS 5:31). Jesus, to Peter and the others in the early church, was the powerful life-saver who made possible the crossing from death to life.

Emphasizing what he had just said about Jesus, Peter stated by way of personal testimony, "And we are witnesses to these things," adding that there is still another Witness, ". . . the Holy Spirit whom God has given to those who obey him." (ACTS 5:32)

The doctrine of the Holy Spirit, to use Winston Churchill's words about Russia, seems to be "a riddle wrapped in a mystery inside an

54

enigma" to many people. "Explain the workings of the Holy Spirit in terms I can understand," laymen frequently plead.

"We are witnesses . . . and so is the Holy Spirit," say the first Christians. The Holy Spirit is the Witness to what God has done. A witness is one who testifies. The Spirit as Witness testifies to the fact of Jesus Christ. He interprets that fact, and personalizes it so that Christians in the first or twenty-first century say, "Now we understand: He hanged on the cross for *us;* He was raised alive for *us.*"

How do we have the testimony of the Witness? Peter's words must be taken in their entirety: "The Holy Spirit whom God has given to *those who obey him.*" Illumination goes with obedience. We receive evidence from the Witness only as we walk by God's promise.

The members of the Council and the Senate were not taking Peter's words in a calm, reasonable way. They were "enraged" (ACTS 5:33), or as the Greek word literally means, "sawn in two." As anger can be a mighty saw tearing a man apart, so these ordinarily staid leaders of Israel were ripped asunder by rage. They wanted to have the Apostles killed on the spot. It is entirely possible that they might have carried out their wishes and made Peter and the other Apostles the first martyrs instead of Stephen had it not been for the intervention of one man—Gamaliel.

Who was Gamaliel? He was the all-time great teacher of Israel, the first of only seven ever to win the title "Rabban," testifying that he was far more highly respected than a regular Rabbi or Rab. Gamaliel enjoyed such respect that once when a motion regarding the determining of a leap year was acted on during his absence from the Council, the measure was passed with the proviso that the proposal would be put into practice only if and when Gamaliel gave his approval.

It took a person with the stature of Gamaliel to speak against the majority and have the Apostles' lives spared. Gamaliel's speech to the Council and Senate that day was a masterpiece of caution and reasonableness. Appealing to well-known recent events in which a series of phony messiahs and abortive uprisings had flared and sputtered, Gamaliel appealed to his cohorts to play it safe. He was too wise to try to stamp out a fanatical movement. Persecution usually fires its followers to bolder deeds. "Let's wait and see," Gamaliel sensibly proposed; "Providence eventually irons out these problems."

Gamaliel's appeal carried the court. Although the disciples were acquitted, they were given a beating before being released. Luke passes over this beating as incidental. It would have been a painful experience, however, for the Apostles: the "thirty-nine stripes" of the lash were not only physically brutal but carried the stigma of public disgrace.

What was the reaction of the disciples to this humiliation and torture? After this last brush with the Jerusalem powers, Jesus' followers *should* have slinked away, licking their wounds. The ordeal had been exhausting and frightening. Did the thought cross their minds to retreat to the desert, or retire to Galilee?

At the tip of the Kerry peninsula, there is a monument to the Irish emancipator, Daniel O'Connell, in which O'Connell's work is summed up by the inscription, "He Found the Irish Peasants Slaves and Left Them Men." These words could also describe the work of the Holy Spirit in the lives of those first Christians. Once enslaved by fear and anxiety, Peter and the other disciples were freed by the Spirit to be creative and confident men.

Cringing and cowed? Snarling for revenge? Not these men! Luke tells us that their mood was one of ". . . rejoicing that they were worthy to suffer dishonor for the name." (ACTS 5:41) They were "dignified by the indignity," as The Amplified New Testament translation puts it. These first Christians remembered the example of Jesus Himself during His humiliation and pain. They were proud to be associated with Him, honored to be able to share His sufferings.

There is in every age a small but blessed band of Christian men and women who have been initiated into the exclusive fellowship of what Calvin described as "companions and sharers of the sufferings of Christ that we may be companions and sharers of His glory."

Sometimes as disciples, we droop and drop. We plead exhaustion. Veterans of a few skirmishes, we think that we are ready for honorable discharge. "I have done my part; it's someone else's turn."

Although the disciples were tempted to think that they, too, had "had enough," they did not retire or retreat. They continued to communicate God's great gift of Jesus Christ.

When? When they felt better; when they could work it into their schedules; when they were in the mood? Where? Out in a desert hideout; under a tree in Galilee; in a university lecture hall?

"And every day in the temple and at home," Luke states, "they did not cease teaching and preaching Jesus as the Christ." (ACTS 5:42)

8

THE FIRST MANIFESTO AND
THE FIRST MARTYR

(ACTS 6 AND 7)

A MEMBERSHIP EXPLOSION WAS ONE OF THE PHENOMENA OF THE early church. Luke tells us at least six times in the first six chapters of Acts that the rolls of the early church grew rapidly (ACTS 2:41; 2:47; 4:4; 5:14; 6:1).

Up until this point, all of these early church members were Jews, albeit with widely differing backgrounds. Many, of course, were Aramaic-speaking natives of Palestine. Others, however, were non-Palestinian, Greek-speaking Jews. Some of these had emigrated to Asia Minor, North Africa or Europe. Others, descended from earliest settlers who had left home in Palestine, were two, three, four, or more generations removed from the homeland.

More at home in Greek than Aramaic, such foreign-born Jews tended to congregate together when visiting Jerusalem. They were called "Hellenists" by the native-born Jews. Slightly looked down upon by the Aramaic-speaking Jews, the Hellenists were thought to be somehow faintly corrupted by their alien culture.

During the membership explosion of the church in Jerusalem, the earliest Christians—all Jews—gravitated into linguistic groups. In one block were the Aramaic speakers, the "Hebrews," the native born "old guard," those who remembered Jesus. The others, the Hellenists, found themselves gathering as a separate congregation, perhaps taking over a Hellenist Jewish synagogue.

Although both the "Hebrews" and the "Hellenists" alike were raised as Jews, and although both received Jesus as the Messiah and Saviour, tension developed between the two which later erupted into conflict and factionalism. Like a surgeon, Luke tries to stitch up the torn parts of the Body, the church, and apply soothing balm to the

57

tender areas. Acts, which plays down the differences between the two parties within the church, is Luke's effort to promote healing.

The first cause of tension was over the care of needy widows from the Hellenist ranks. Luke has pointed out earlier that the early Jerusalem church tried to look after Christians in hardship. As the numbers increased, this became more and more difficult and inevitably, there were complaints that some were being neglected. Some sort of organizational machinery was needed.

The Twelve, apparently deferred to as a "board" by the rest of the Jerusalem Christians during the church's infancy, readily saw the problem. They also knew that they had neither the time nor temperament for administration, and said, "It is not right that we should give up preaching the word of God to serve tables." (ACTS 6:2)

"To serve tables" alludes to the money-changers' tables, referring to finances. In other words, the Apostles were urging that able men be chosen to handle the the business side of the church's affairs. These administrators, however, were not selected to oil the machinery but to serve the poor. Because this idea of service was stressed, those chosen are popularly known as the first "deacons" (the word deacon means literally "one who serves") although they were not actually designated by that title in Luke's account.

The Hellenist group elected seven of their number, ". . . men of good repute, full of the Spirit and of wisdom. . . ." (ACTS 6:3) It is interesting that these three traits of honesty, spirituality, and wisdom are exactly the qualities that the Pharoah saw that Joseph had. (GENESIS 41:38-39) Why seven? Was it because they divided Jerusalem into seven districts and wished to put one man in each as an area captain? Or, did they arrange to have one man in charge of the distribution to the needy on each of the seven days in the week?

Who were these seven administrators of the Poor Fund? They were all laymen, not "religious professionals." Continuing the tradition begun by Jesus in calling fishermen and tax-collectors to His ranks, the early church was a lay movement.

It is worthwhile to note that the Seven were selected by the entire group, not by the Twelve, not by Peter, not by any ruling clique. Further evidence of the lay character of the church in its beginning is found in the "ordination" service for the Seven. No coronation elevated the Seven to a higher standing; it was simply giving these men a commission, appointing them to a task.

In appointing the Seven, the church introduced a practice which has been used ever since in ordaining people to a specific responsibility: the laying on of hands. Long used in Israel in commissioning rabbis, laying on of hands represented the bestowal of spiritual gifts by God through the community upon the man being ordained. Later, as we shall note in Acts, laying on of hands came to be associated with the giving of the Holy Spirit. In the service for the Seven, the laying on of the hands was identical with Jewish usage. The worshipping community recognized certain individuals and appointed them to certain responsibilities.

The names of the Seven: Stephen, Philip, Prochorus, Nicanor, Timon, Parmenas, and Nicolaus. Of this group, only two—Stephen and Philip—achieved any prominence. Neither Luke nor any other New Testament writer ever refers again to the other five. What happened to Prochorus, Nicanor, Timon, Parmenas, and Nicolaus? No awards, no mention in later dispatches for them. Undoubtedly, these five continued doing a quiet but necessary job of looking after the poor. Philip and Stephen became flaming orators, as we shall note. Necessary though Philip and Stephen were for the advance of the gospel, there was also need for their five unrecognized, undistinguished brothers. The Holy Spirit uses gifts of the Prochoruses—the ordinary privates like most of us—as well as those of the Stephens!

With the commissioning of the Seven, a new chapter opened in the history of the church. Earlier, the Holy Spirit had vitalized a small core of Jesus' followers. Through this tiny company, the Spirit in turn affected a larger group, all Jews, but including many Hellenists. The Hellenists who welcomed Jesus as the Christ proved to be more aggressive and imaginative than those who had introduced them to the gospel. This group steps into the foreground while Peter and the Apostles gradually recede in importance in the remainder of Acts.

When the congregation of Greek-speaking, non-Palestinian ex-Jews was asked to order its own affairs by the Apostles, two of the leaders, Stephen and Philip, interpreted their assignment as more than looking after the finances. If the church was to be true to Jesus' orders, they believed, it meant missionary responsibilities.

Stephen who carried the gospel into other Greek-speaking Jewish synagogues, was both a persuasive speaker and a powerful worker of "wonders and signs among the people." (ACTS 6:8) His crusade resulted in disruption in these synagogues and deeper antagonism from the established powers. With feeling rising against the church, it is not surprising that Stephen soon became a marked man, arrested and arraigned on trumped-up double charges of blasphemy and treason.

Stephen's defense before the High Priest and the Council is such a brilliant exposition of the meaning of the gospel that Luke includes it in its entirety (ACTS 7:2-53). The speech, a clearly-reasoned masterpiece outlining the church's tie with the Old Testament community, was quoted as the earliest Christian "propaganda piece," the first manifesto of the New Covenant.

We have already seen that Peter's addresses reflected the conviction that the church was a continuation of God's chosen nation, Israel. Stephen developed this idea fully. Beginning with God's call to Abraham, Stephen meticulously traced the history of Israel, pointing out how, through the nation's startling survival, God has had a purpose in mind. This purpose has finally been summed up and fulfilled, Stephen announced, with the "coming of the Righteous One." (ACTS 7:52). Throughout his address, Stephen skillfully showed that this Righteous One has been promised by God throughout the long story of Israel's remarkable existence, and quoted the greatest eminent, Moses, in Deuteronomy 18:15-18, stating, "God will raise up for you a prophet from your brethern as he raised me up." (ACTS 7:37)

"Forget about the Old Testament," we hear sometimes today. "What does the story of Abraham and Moses have to do with us? Let's stick to the New Testament. After all, isn't that all we need?"

This viewpoint was presented most forcefully and articulately about a century after Stephen by a wealthy shipowner named Marcion who became a Christian and came to Rome about A.D. 139. Marcion disowned the church's debt to Israel. He even repudiated the authority of the Old Testament, claiming that these had nothing to do with the meaning of Jesus. Marcion put together a collection of Scripture, but left his "Bible" curiously shorn of all references to God's acts prior to Jesus.

The church recognized the fallacy and the danger of amputating Jesus and His church from their Jewish background. After repeatedly asking Marcion to desist from spreading his mistaken notions, the church was finally forced to state in A.D. 144 that Marcion was guilty of spreading heresy and division.

Although the Marcionites hung on as a sect only until the fifth century A.D., the church has never quite succeeded in getting Marcion's ideas out of its hair. Even today, there are Christians who disavow any tie to Israel. Neo-Marcionites appear in every generation.

Martin Luther, aware of these unwitting heretics, as usual answers them in homely but effective terms: "The Old Testament is the cradle in which the Christ child is laid."

Far from being irrelevant or superfluous, our Old Testament heritage explains New Testament history. Our faith in Jesus Christ is rooted in God's dealings with the nation of Israel.

Until Stephen, every believer had accepted the gospel—*and* the law *and* the temple. Securely locked in the ancient traditions, the "Hebrews" in the church preserved—even idealized—all the time-honored institutions of the past. Although they sincerely believed in Jesus, they were actually Christian Jews rather than Jewish Christians.

Stephen was the first to see that the temple trappings, ceremonials and rules could be dispensed with. In effect, Stephen challenged the community of God's people to go forward. Israel, Stephen made clear, could leave the safe, traditional paths and trust the living Spirit to guide it. God's great breakthrough of grace through Jesus Christ was not an added feature to the old ordinances and practices of Judaism, a postscript stuck on the Old Testament. Jesus Christ, not the temple and its lore, is meant to be worshiped.

If Stephen's words upset some churchmen, they infuriated the members of the Sanhedrin. "They were enraged," Luke tells us (ACTS 7:54) and his word "enraged" in Greek means snarling and snapping like wild dogs. The normally sedate, stuffy Sanhedrin completely forgot its dignity. The only person on the scene who was unperturbed was Stephen.

Pointblank, Stephen told his nation's religious leaders that they, like all their predecessors, had conceitedly thought that they had a monopoly on God's favors. These favors, they mistakenly assumed, were obtained through the trappings of temple ceremonial, but Stephen seared his listeners by emphasizing that the temple and its rituals were all man-made and impermanent. Israel, Stephen declared, has always been stubborn, has always thought it knew all about salvation. In truth, in age after age, it had rejected every God-sent messenger. Stephen wound up his address by telling his accusers that they had not ony been ignorant of the real meaning of Israel's history but had been guilty of murdering the Promised Saviour.

The uproar that broke loose almost cut off Stephen's words. Many readers are so caught up in the hubbub within the Sanhedrin that they overlook Stephen's concluding sentence, the key which opens a dramatically different dimension in the church's theology, and marks the beginning of a radically new thrust in the church's mission. The sentence: "Behold, I see the heavens opened, and the Son of man standing at the right hand of God." (ACTS 7:56)

What about this phrase "the Son of man?" Significantly, it was used by Stephen *and no one else* except Jesus in the New Testament. Stephen saw what the others had missed: Jesus is the Messiah in more than the narrow Jewish sense, Jesus is the *world* Messiah. Jesus has more significance than merely the Anointed Deliverer of the Jews. Jesus' life, death, and resurrection, Stephen understood, have world-wide implications.

Stephen's speech is the prototype of all later orthodox Christian theology. No one ever suspected that one of those snarling and snapping the loudest at Stephen's trial, an angry young Pharisee named Saul, would some day pick up Stephen's ideas and develop them into the great doctrine embodied in the words, "Therefore, since we are justified by faith, we have peace with God through our Lord Jesus Christ." (ROMANS 5:1)

We wonder what else Stephen might have had to say that day before the Sanhedrin. We also wonder what other speeches and writing this outstanding young Hellenist might have left us had his life been spared. But one thing is certain—after his brief but brilliant career, the church was never the same again. Stephen's testimony was the seed for the next great growth-surge of the church. In embryo, his words contained the ideas which eventually broke the church out of the husk of a sect in the temple. Stephen was the thinker and the witness used by the Spirit to propel the church out of Jerusalem into the world.

On the other hand, Stephen's activities accented the uneasiness between the Hellenists and the "Hebrews." Many of the latter, although acknowledging Jesus as the Christ, were ultra-conservative, rigid Levitical types who reacted nervously to Stephen's suggestion to move beyond the temple. Some of these, unwilling to be led by the Spirit, ultimately hardened into a faction of troublemakers which insisted that to be a Christian, one must first be circumcised as a Jew. We shall hear much of this crew in our study of Acts.

Stephen's last words before the Sanhedrin were lost in the exploding uproar. There was no vote, no death sentence. What followed was a mob scene, a lynching. Luke does not say whether the Sanhedrin—always a stickler for the Law—threw the rules to the wind or whether it tried unsuccessfully to control the tumult. Nor is there any mention of the Roman authorities. Was Pilate under such criticism that he looked the other way? Or had he already been suspended and his successor, Marcellus, not arrived?

62

Stephen was brutally dragged through the streets, swung by the arms and legs by the chanting mob, heaved out over a drop-off, bombarded with heavy rocks until he was knocked senseless and eventually died. Before his death, however, Stephen did two notable things.

The first was to pray, "Lord Jesus, receive my spirit." (ACTS 7:59) The tense of the verb in the Greek indicates that Stephen was praying these words over and over.

Notice that Stephen was continually addressing *Jesus,* the first example of direct prayer to Him. Stephen reinforced his conviction that Jesus is God-come-to-him, the world Messiah. Prayer to Jesus is prayer to God.

The second notable thing that Stephen did was to kneel and beg God's forgiveness upon his tormenters and killers. "Lord," Stephen cried in his agony, "Do not hold this sin against them." (ACTS 7:60)

Luke, who could never forget how Jesus had gasped a prayer for the forgiveness of his executers, was the only gospel writer to remember the words from the cross, "Father, forgive them; for they know not what they do." (LUKE 23:34) Luke the doctor knew the healing power of the Great Physician's prayer, and recognized the echo of it in Stephen's last words.

"For men use, if they have an evil tourne, to write it in marble; and whoso doth us a good tourne we write it in duste," wrote Sir Thomas More in the stormy sixteenth century. His observation of human nature is astute; men do tend to forget good turns and remember vividly the hurts and evil done them. The game of life is a grudge match for most.

The early Christians escaped writing the evil turns of others "in marble." The Holy Spirit, no one else, accomplished the miracle of transforming Stephen and the others into forgiving men.

9

TRUMPETERS TO THE STRANGERS

(ACTS 8)

A MISSIONARY TO EGYPT TOLD AN AMERICAN AUDIENCE HOW A FEL-
low missionary had heard the desperate cries for help of an Arab
Moslem child in the water, had dashed into the surf to attempt a
rescue, but had drowned. The Moslem youngster survived.

Hearing of the missionary's sacrifice, one member of the audience
snorted, "So pointless!"

What did Stephen's death accomplish? Undoubtedly, there were
those who were convinced that his witness was pointless. For one
thing, Stephen's speech and death triggered a persecution. Although
the threat of arrest and imprisonment had hung over the Christian
community, everyone was stunned when the avalanche fell.

For another thing, Stephen's public testimony unleashed the anger
of one particular investigator, Saul of Tarsus. Saul's hate for everything Christian apparently knew no limits, and he began to do everything humanly possible to extinguish the church.

The uneasiness between the Hellenists and the "Hebrews" in the
church was deepened when the brunt of the persecution fell on the
Hellenists, who were forced to flee for their lives while the Apostles
were able to remain. Naturally, those losing property and being
hounded were suspicious toward those who were spared. Had those
who had escaped arrest gone underground? Or had they been by-
passed in the manhunt because the authorities wanted only the trou-
blesome Hellenists? In any case, a wedge appeared between those who
suffered and those who had not. Some of the more conservative
"Hebrews" became skeptical of the way that the Hellenists seemed to
be assuming the initiative in the church. A few even began to grumble
that the Greek-speaking Christians were starting to "take over" the
church. The troubles following Stephen's stoning only watered the
seeds of antagonism.

Stephen's crusade and death seemed to do nothing except crush the

65

church. All plans were upset. The persecution scattered believers and ripped apart the fragile organization. "A martyr—for what?" many probably thought. "Look at how the church has been ruined."

But the Holy Spirit is never blockaded. He takes situations which seem to be setbacks, changes them into setups for new witnessing, and even uses those who oppose Him.

The persecuters thought that they were crushing the young church. Unwittingly, these oppressors became the very cause of the spread of the gospel! Like stamping on embers only to have the sparks fly out and ignite a ring of new fires, the persecution scattered believers throughout Judea and Samaria who quickly set the gospel blazing among people everywhere. The Holy Spirit used the opposition to trigger the first missionary movement.

Even today, in the face of opposition from without the church, in reply to "God-is-dead" talk from within the church, the Spirit is at work. He may give the church a radical new form, even as He did when persecution strewed Hellenists believers across the Palestine countryside. Every time the world has cleared its throat to pronounce the church dead, the Spirit has stirred the body to startling new life.

The Spirit used Stephen's death to teach the church a lesson. It is significant that the word "martyr" in Greek means "witness." Through the Spirit, the church began to understand that even the act of dying, rather than being pointless, can be a form of witness. Tertellian, an early church father (A.D. 160-240), said it most memorably: "The blood of the martyrs is the seed of the church."

On July 6, 1415, a peasant-born theologian-preacher in Bohemia named John Hus was put to death for exalting the Bible and protesting corruption in the church. Few realized at the time that Hus was anticipating the Reformation, and some thought his testimony and death foolish. What seeds this brave Bohemian's blood planted! It took a century for them to flower, but by February, 1520, Martin Luther referred to himself as "the Saxon Hus."

Stephen's witness planted the meaning of the church in the lives of his fellow Hellenist Christians. Although no one realized it at the time, the leadership of the church shifted from the Apostles and "Hebrews" to these energetic, imaginative young men. From this point on in Acts, the importance of Jerusalem dims. Stephen's martyrdom burst the church from its temple husk, exploding his associates into Samaria, Judea, the Philistine coast, Antioch, Cyprus, Asia Minor —even Europe!

Stephen's death was the seed of the world mission of the church.

Led by Philip, one of "the Seven," this audacious crew "went about preaching the word" (ACTS 8:4) or, as the Greek says literally, "bringing good news." Evangelizing or "bringing good news" is one of Luke's most common themes—one of his favorite words. This Greek verb, used only once in the other gospel accounts (MATTHEW 11:5) is used by Luke at least ten times in his Gospel and at least fifteen times in Acts!

Luke the "outsider," remembering that somebody had brought the good news to him, never let the church forget its call to evangelize strangers. Acts is in a sense a propaganda piece to push the church into the world.

Luke illustrates his point with the story of Philip, who shattered all tradition by going to the non-Jewish areas of Samaria and the Philistine coast.

What a radical departure to go to Samaritans! Respectable Jews shunned Samaritans as riff-raff—half-way Jews who stubbornly hung on to the watered-down beliefs and second class worship of their heretical fathers 500 years earlier.

Philip, knowing that God sent Jesus Christ for Samaritans as well as Jews, broke the pattern hitherto established of preaching only to Jews. He "proclaimed to them the Christ." (ACTS 8:5) No timid whispers here. Luke's Greek states that Philip "heralded" the good news as a royal envoy boldly trumpets an imperial proclamation.

The church had phenomenal success in Samaria. Philip's preaching and cures even impressed a real somebody in Samaria, a superstitious dealer in spells and charms named Simon. Every Oriental town had a handful of fakirs who made a good living dabbling in astrology and dispensing magic. Simon of Samaria was king of the magicians there. Simon, who recognized a man of power when he saw one, knew that Philip had something that no magician had; he promptly signed up as a "Christian." Luke adds a long footnote on Simon to illustrate (a) how the early evangelists out-cured all local magicians; (b) how the Holy Spirit is more powerful than any brand of magic.

Meanwhile, word seeped back to Jerusalem of the startling evangelism program by the Hellenist Christians among the Samaritans. The conservative Apostles were uneasy. Others in the Jerusalem church were jarred. Carrying the gospel to Samaritans was casting pearls before swine.

The Jerusalem group nervously decided to elect a two-man team to look into the strange goings-on, and sent off Peter and John. Their

67

orders, although not spelled out, were understood as follows: to check whether or not the Samaritan conversions were genuine; to forge a bond between any new Christians and the Jerusalem church; to make certain that all new followers knew the working of the Holy Spirit.

Peter and John quickly discovered that Philip and other evangelists were effective trumpeters to Samaria. Although many had been baptized, Peter and John added the "extra" of laying their hands on the heads of new converts. Some have tried to interpret this action as a conferring of the Holy Spirit by the Apostles. Peter and John were not regarded as the exclusive agents of the Spirit, nor were they making a "bishops' tour" to confirm new members. The Greek verb form of ACTS 8:17 is the imperfect tense, saying in effect that Peter and John were continually laying their hands on new Samaritan Christians and that during their visit, new Christians were time after time receiving the gift of the Spirit. Luke, apparently not holding any of the Apostles in any great veneration, never mentions John again by name in Acts.

During Peter's and John's visit, new wonders were done by the Holy Spirit. Simon, the magician who had been so impressed by Philip's signs of power, was even more awed by Peter and John. Simon had bought many "secrets" from clever charlatans and added them to his stock of tricks, and Peter's "Holy Spirit" looked like one more. Thinking that Peter was probably just one more dealer in the black arts like himself, Simon sidled up and asked how much Peter wanted for his "Holy Spirit."

In salty, fishermen prose, Peter told Simon exactly where he could go with such a request. The Holy Spirit, Peter stated, is not some mysterious force to be manipulated, not a trick to amuse the crowds. The source of Peter's power lay not in his hands but beyond.

The word "simony," meaning trafficking in sacred matters, comes from this greedy, superstitious fake with the superficial faith. Although we associate the term with medieval church corruption, we are guilty of simony any time we try to exploit the Holy Spirit.

Peter's scorching words to Simon apply also to us whenever we try to manipulate the Spirit for our own profit and comfort: "You are in the gall of bitterness and in the bond of iniquity." (ACTS 8:23)

Whether Simon's repentance was from fear or from faith we cannot judge. He did, however, plead with Peter to keep anything horrible from happening to him.

Peter and John caught the enthusiasm and energy of the Hellenist

Christians in preaching to outsiders. Exhilarated by the Spirit, the two Apostles deliberately stopped in Samaritan villages to preach the gospel. Evangelism, in the early church, was not a sideline or a speciality—it was the business of every believer, wherever he went, with whomever he met.

Luke amply illustrates this. He switches back to Philip. This time, we find Philip on the Gaza Road, a man on the move, on fire to tell the good news.

The tempo of the march of the Spirit was speeding up, pushing over one barrier after another. A short while ago, there seemed to be a barrier against Greek-speaking, non-Palestinian Jews in the church. The Spirit toppled that barrier, brought in Stephen, Philip, and the Hellenists. Then there was the barrier against Samaritans. Suddenly, that barrier, too, meant nothing. Other barriers, however, remained in the church. The next to fall was that against foreigners, when Philip baptized an Ethiopian. At least Samaritans were distantly related by blood ties and common traditions. Not so with Ethiopians—Philip brought a complete outsider into the church.

This was not a whim from the mind of Philip, not an enlightened policy from a council of churchmen. The instructions came from outside, "Go up," the Spirit commanded Philip, "and join this chariot." (ACTS 8:29)

Real evangelism starts with what the Holy Spirit asks. We recognize that He initiates. We participate. He terminates.

"*Join* this chariot," Philip is told, or literally, *glue yourself* to this man! Here is the difference between Christian evangelism and religious revivalism. The evangelist sees the other as a person, not as a statistic, cares about the other as a person, means to stay with him, understand him, listen to him, speak with him. The revivalist treats the other as an audience to be addressed and then left, but the evangelist regards him as a brother to be met and loved.

"What does your Christian friend do for you?" sneered a fellow patient to the bedfast indigent in the "hopeless" ward. "She comes and she sits," whispered the second, "and she cries with me." He knew the blessings of the evangelist who glued herself to a lonely, ill person.

Philip's man was Secretary of the Treasury in the Ethiopian government. Cabinet officer or candle-maker, to Philip the Ethiopian was simply another man in need of help. In typical Oriental fashion, the official was reading aloud, chanting Isaiah 53:7-8 from a scroll he had probably just bought at great expense in Jerusalem.

69

Philip met the man on his own ground. "Do you understand what you are reading?" (ACTS 8:30) he asked.

The Ethiopian treasurer's answer is a mandate for Christian teaching, from Sunday schools to seminaries. He asked, 'How can I, unless someone guides me?' "And he invited Philip to come up and sit with him" (ACTS 8:31).

Philip began at the point where the Ethiopian already was, using this as the starting place for the dialogue which would end, as eventually every dialogue did, with questions about Jesus Christ.

Church people are sometimes guilty of refusing to meet others where they are, too frequently failing to join in conversation with the world. Unwilling to listen, we interrupt with what *we* want to say. In turn, others grow irritated, snap, "The church is irrelevant."

"You say that Christ is the answer," one teenaged troublemaker told a pastor visiting him in Juvenile Court. "Well," the boy challenged, "what's the question?" The pastor suddenly realized that he had not given the boy a chance to ask any question, had not tried to meet the boy on his own ground, had not given him the dignity of hearing what he had to say before handing him a churchy cliché.

Philip truly earned his title, "the Evangelist," by meeting the other as a person, right where he was, and not imposing a ready-made pronouncement or re-preaching last week's sermon. Somehow, the church is in the habit of thinking that evangelism is a hit-and-run matter. With revivalism, yes. But evangelism, no. Proclaiming the gospel implies careful teaching, patient explaining, long-term educating. The most effective Christian evangelist will perhaps be a teacher toiling with a class week by week rather than a flashy visiting pulpit-pounder.

Working through the Isaiah passage which puzzled the Ethiopian, Philip and he together reached a new insight into the meaning of Jesus Christ. Philip was a model evangelist: teacher as well as preacher. He set the pattern for effective evangelism: profound instruction as well as moving testimony.

Recently Henry Bucher, a missionary at Petburi, Thailand, found the diary of an unknown early missionary. Dating back to the 1870's, the diary describes how the writer had "evangelized" Bucher's area of Thailand, stopping briefly to preach in various towns, immediately baptizing converts, then going on to the next place. In one entry, the diary keeper boasts that his quick visit to the village of Bangtaloo had instantly resulted in a new congregation of twenty—larger than any other congregation anywhere in Thailand at that time!

Henry Bucher, who had worked for years near Bangtaloo, had never heard of any Christian congregation there. Nevertheless, he carefully interviewed nearly every family in Bangtaloo. He could not find one Christian, nor could he find anyone who could even remember a congregation there.

What happened to the church that disappeared in Bangtaloo? Simply this: the missionary in the 1870's had a superficial understanding of evangelism, failing to realize that the church must teach as well as preach. There had been no careful instruction or follow-up, only a quick speech or two, hasty baptisms and departure.

The church must teach or die. Without deepening knowledge, evangelism declines into cheap revivalism.

Philip brought the Ethiopian to a point of personal decision before Jesus Christ, the purpose of all evangelism. Christianity without commitment is empty.

Some ancient manuscripts include the Ethiopian official's statement of faith: "I believe that Jesus Christ is the Son of God." (ACTS 8:37) Here is the church's earliest creed. After twenty centuries, these words are still *the* basic article of faith!

Philip did more than bring the Ethiopian to Jesus Christ—he baptized him into the church, knowing that the new convert would need encouragement, support, and instruction in the faith from the Christian community.

Eusebius, the early church historian, states that the Ethiopian, whose name was Indich, became an active leader in the ancient church. According to Eusebius, Indich caught the meaning of evangelism and bore the good news of Jesus Christ to his homeland.

Luke records that Philip continued his evangelistic activities first at Azotus (the ancient Philistine city of Ashdod) among the outsiders there, and working through other towns of the area until he came to his home at Caesarea. Whether carried on by Philip, the Ethiopian cabinet officer, or anyone else in the church, evangelism was a "do-it-yourself" project for every Christian.

71

10

SURPRISE AT DAMASCUS

(ACTS 9: 1-30)

SOMETIMES A TRIVIAL EVENT WILL PLANT AN IDEA-TIME-BOMB IN the mind of a person which may take months or years to detonate.

Abraham Lincoln remembered the horror which he felt when he saw his first slave auction in New Orleans after a flatboat trip down the Mississippi. The year was 1831—thirty-two years before he signed the Emancipation Proclamation—but the incident ignited Lincoln's thinking.

Albert Schweitzer recalled how, as a well-fed pastor's son in Alsace, he once bested a poor boy from the village in wrestling. Between sobs, his undernourished adversary taunted, "Sure, you get broth every day!" Twenty-three years later, determined to minister to the have-nots in the world, Schweitzer forsook fame and sailed to equatorial Africa.

Bleeding Stephen's words and demeanor eventually meant the end of a promising career for a young fire-breather of a Pharisee named Saul and the beginning of the ministry of one of history's most capable, committed, and colorful personalities, Paul the Apostle.

Saul's home town was Tarsus, located at the corner where Asia Minor joins Syria. It was a distinguished city: its university, one of the top three, ranked with Athens and Alexandria as the Harvard, Yale, and Princeton of the day; its crowded wharves on the Cydnus River made it a bustling cosmopolitan center.

Saul's father, a Roman citizen, passed on this priceless asset to his son. Again, through his Pharisee father, Saul could match credentials with the most ardent Jew. In keeping with Jewish tradition that a boy should know a trade, young Saul was taught to weave cloth from black goat hair and fashion it into strips for tents.

At about thirteen, Saul was packed off to Jerusalem to study to be a rabbi. His teacher, Gamaliel, was so revered as a paragon of enlightenment and toleration that he was called "the Beauty of the

73

Law." Saul's course under Gamaliel included years of memorizing Scripture and intensive question-answer periods on the law.

Since he never mentioned ever meeting Jesus during His earthly ministry, it is possible that Saul returned to Tarsus and held a synagogue office there for a few years.

The rigid young Saul was back in Jerusalem by the time Stephen and a large number of Hellenist Jews were acclaiming Jesus. When these aggressive new Christians tried to persuade others to join their fellowship, Saul was angry. He tried to refute them, but they were unshakable. Foiled in debate, Saul joined others in grabbing other weapons, and he was present when they silenced Stephen with stones.

What did Saul think after Stephen's death? Did he try to convince himself that he was technically "innocent," that he had not actually *thrown* any stones? Did he reassure himself that he was only a bystander who had guarded the coats of the participants?

Saul became the inquisitor, dedicated to silencing Stephen's point of view. Years later he testified, "I myself was convinced that I ought to do many things in opposing the name of Jesus of Nazareth. And I did so in Jerusalem; I not only shut up many of the saints in prison, by authority from the chief priests, but when they were put to death I cast my vote against them. And I punished them often in all the synagogues and tried to make them blaspheme; and in raging fury against them, I persecuted them even to foreign cities." (ACTS 26:9-11)

Saul's crusading zeal against Christians, we note by these words, earned him a seat on the illustrious Sanhedrin—a signal honor for a man in his early thirties.

Luke tells us that Saul "laid waste the church," and uses the Greek word describing a wild boar rampaging through a garden or an army devastating a city. Only an uneasy, insecure or desperate man resorts to violence. "If I cannot bring you to my position by argument, I'll do it by force," sums up his thinking. Saul betrayed how insecure in his beliefs he was by trying to remove all who disagreed with him.

After successfully clearing Jerusalem of all heretics, he started to hunt out pockets of hated Christians everywhere. Hearing of the appearance of a group in Damascus, Saul secured permission to ransack the Jewish community there. His commission gave him almost umlimited powers: extradite all Christians hiding in Damascus; root out of the synagogues any with sympathies toward Christians or leanings toward the church.

From Jerusalem to Damascus the best route ran north through Shechem, Samaria and Galilee, and Saul probably took this road. He would have been infuriated to have seen the inroads of the church among the Samaritan villages, and perhaps toyed with the idea of stopping to search and arrest in Samaria. Saul, however, was after big game. Damascus, seat of an enormous Jewish community (so large that during Nero's terror, ten thousand Jews were put to death in Damascus alone!), was more of a troublespot than Samaritan villages. He could mop these up later. Saul went tornadoing north. So intent was he to get to Damascus that he would not even stop during the midday heat when all sensible travelers rested. Saul was plunging toward Damascus under the noon sun when his dramatic conversion occurred.

Caravans always allowed at least six days' traveling time from Jerusalem to Damascus. In spite of his hurry, Saul had to spend about a week on the road. He had an opportunity for thought and reflection for the first time since Stephen's death. A crisis was brewing in Saul's life. He undoubtedly recalled Stephen's words. He probably guiltily remembered the big-hearted toleration of Gamaliel, his great teacher. The route led to Damascus through Galilee, and Saul must have remembered that this was the home country of the Person who was the cause of his unrest. As he hurried along the road through Galilee, did Saul think of the name by which Christianity was called at that time: "the Way"—or, literally, "the Road" (ACTS 9:2)? Did Saul ponder how these Christians referred to the gospel of Jesus Christ as "the Road" because Jesus once said, "I am the way, and the truth, and the life; no one comes to the Father, but by me?" (JOHN 14:6)

A flash. So terrifyingly sudden that it hurled everyone in Saul's party to the ground. So blinding that Saul could not see.

A voice. "Saul, Saul, why do you persecute me?" (ACTS 9:4)

Saul replied. "Who are you, Lord?" (ACTS 9:5) "Lord" in this sense means the same as "sir," and is the respectful form of address in classical Greek for a god, king, or master of a household, implying that Saul at first thought that one of his victims was speaking.

The Voice again. "I am Jesus, whom you are persecuting." (ACTS 9:5)

The words were simple, direct. "I am Jesus." Not a booming announcement, "I am the Everlasting and Almighty Son of God, the Eternal Word made flesh."

In the twentieth century, when it is popular to psychologize everything, some try to analyze Saul's Damascus Road experience as a case history. Tormented though Saul was, he was not a susceptible dupe and it is not correct to state that he was swept off his feet by mental fancy or a "vision."

Saul himself insisted that the experience was not subjectivism but the last of Jesus' resurrection appearances. In reading the accounts of Saul's conversion in Acts 9, Acts 22, Acts 26, I Corinthians 15:3-11, and Galatians 1:13-21, the point is made repeatedly that the Risen Christ encountered Saul that day, not that some mysterious, ecstatic experience occurred to Saul.

God does not always intervene in such dramatic ways. It is presumptious for anyone to decide how God calls any person.

Saul, later writing as the Christian Paul, flatly refused to amplify on either details or discussions of Damascus road experiences. In II CORINTHIANS 12:1, he concedes that there are "visions and revelations of the Lord" which have been granted to him. However satisfying these private experiences may be, he does not blare about them. In fact, in I CORINTHIANS 14:18, Paul is reticent even to talk about the subject because it really does not help others to grow as Christians. Dwelling on details of emotional experiences can turn one into a spiritual snob, separating one from the rest of the believers. If it was not appropriate to Paul to spill all the intriguing minutiae of his "secret" or "private" call, neither is it appropriate for us to insist that others do it—or that we do it ourselves.

The details of Saul's Damascus Road experience are irrelevant; the point is that the Lord, who chose Saul before Saul chose the Lord, addressed Saul. The inquisitor was transformed into the apostle.

At last, there would be peace for Saul. It would be a long life of tension and heartache, but at the center was the calm certainty that he stood before God as a forgiven man.

Saul's entry into Damascus was entirely different from what he had planned. Submissive instead of strutting, taking orders instead of giving them, the blinded ex-tormenter was led by the hand.

For three days, Saul sat stunned, helpless, friendless. His associates would give him no sympathy. The Christians, terrified, were afraid to come near. Saul had to endure his ordeal of blindness alone; a blackness that was emotional as well as physical. As he remembered Stephen and others he had tortured, Saul must have groaned with remorse. As he thought of the voice of Jesus on the Damascus road, Saul must have been tempted to doubt, to ask if it had not been a fantasy. Men's minds do strange things after a few hours of lonely, silent darkness.

What would the future be? Recalling Jesus' final words on the Damascus road, Saul must have been unsettled. Jesus seemed to leave things hanging; ". . . Enter the city and you will be told what you are to do." (ACTS 9:6) When? By whom?

Saul during his three days of misery learned that Jesus left His followers with a promise, not with proofs. Once seething, now subdued, Saul began to understand that obeying Jesus meant walking by faith.

Jesus kept His word. As He frequently does, He carried out His promise in an unexpected way, sending an inconspicuous unknown named Ananias to befriend Saul.

Obviously Ananias had never met Saul before, and knowing Saul's reputation, he was reluctant to stick his neck out—admitting you were a Christian to Saul had been the same as signing your own death-warrant. In spite of the risk, Ananias sought the stranger Saul and greeted him trustingly as *"Brother* Saul" (ACTS 9:17) at a time when no one else would go near him.

Discipleship means risks. God Himself took the greatest risks at the cross and resurrection. What proof did He have that He could ever penetrate our hostility or apathy? Here is a fundamental difference between Christianity and every "religion." The Christian takes risks for others because God risked everything for mankind.

Luke the doctor, using the medical term for particles or scaly substances given off by the body, writes that when Ananias laid his hands on Saul, ". . . . something like scales fell from his eyes." (ACTS 9:18) Saul regained his sight and was baptized. Perhaps Luke means that more than the encrustation came loose so that Saul could see again. Baptism in the early church was sometimes called "illumination," and Saul was given the gift of seeing in more ways than one when the Spirit sent Ananias to him.

With the practicality that typifies Christianity, Luke mentions that Saul ". . . took food and was strengthened." (ACTS 9:19) Christians have always had a concern for everyday human needs, for bodies as well as souls.

Luke is not writing a full-scale biography of Saul. Although he gives three accounts of Saul's conversion (ACTS 9, ACTS 22 and ACTS 26), Luke capsulizes the story, skipping many details of Saul's career between his conversion and his first interview with the Apostles in Jerusalem. To fill in the gaps we can turn to GALATIANS 1:13-21. Saul

77

(writing as Paul) tells us specifically that he left Damascus, went to "Arabia" (which can mean either the Sinai area or Petra), presumably for a period of contemplation, and then returned to Damascus.

Saul immediately plunged in to preach about Jesus. Faith is never a "private" matter; Saul boldly and publicly announced what Jesus meant. His former cronies, furious, marked him for extermination as a turncoat. Saul's breathtaking escape by night from Damascus could be titled "Over the wall in a basket."

GALATIANS 1:18 says that this was three years after Saul's conversion; ACTS 9:23 states that it was "When many days had passed." There is no discrepancy, however. Luke's mention of "many days" is a Hebraic term meaning years, an example being found in I KINGS 2:38-39 where the phrase equals three years.

Saul came to Jerusalem, where, despite the lapse in time, his former reputation clung to him. When he tried to meet with the Christians in Jerusalem, ". . . they were all afraid of him for they did not believe that he was a disciple." (ACTS 9:26) Understandably, they suspected him of being an undercover agent, an imposter, or at best a flighty enthusiast.

Again, a great-hearted believer stepped forward to lay life and reputation on the line and stand up for Saul. In Damascus, it was Ananias; in Jerusalem, Barnabas. The suspicions and uneasiness were dispelled. Luke recounts, "So he went in and out among them . . ." (ACTS 9:28), using the Hebrew expression meaning that Saul was accepted by the Apostles as a close friend and familiar associate.

Saul tried to make whatever amends he could for his past. As Stephen's replacement, he took up the cause he had once fought, visiting the same synagogues where Stephen had spoken, "preaching boldly in the name of the Lord." (ACTS 9:29)

Quickly, things became too hot for Saul in Jerusalem. The Apostles, regarding themselves by now as Saul's "brethren" (ACTS 9:30), smuggled him out of Jerusalem to the port of Caesarea to escape the vengeful authorities, hustling him aboard a ship bound for his home, Tarsus.

What kind of a reception did Saul get in Tarsus? Were his stern, Pharisee father (if still alive), family, and friends ashamed, disgusted, or hurt? Did they pressure Saul to recant? Did they write him off?

During the next years, Saul actively worked with the church in Tarsus and his home province. Perhaps he made some converts in his own family: mention of his nephew in ACTS 23:17-23 hints that his sister and her family might have become Christians or at least sympathetic to "the Way."

While it was a period of marking time for Saul, The Spirit was still at work. The last barrier was about to crumble. Gentiles were to be included in the church. The Spirit was preparing the Apostles in Jerusalem for this radical and momentous step.

11

THE DAY THE HORIZON STRETCHED

(ACTS 9: 31-11:18)

"BUT, HUCK, WE CAN'T LET YOU INTO THE GANG IF YOU AIN'T respectable, you know."

Huck's joy was quenched.

"Can't let me in, Tom? Didn't you let me go for a pirate?"

"Yes, but that's different. A robber is more high-toned than what a pirate is—as a general thing. In most countries, they're awful high up in the nobility—dukes and such."

"Now, Tom, hain't you always been friendly to me? You wouldn't shut me out, would you, Tom? You wouldn't do that, now, *would* you, Tom?"

"Huck, I wouldn't want to, and I *don't* want to—but what would people say? Why, they'd say, 'Mph! Tom Sawyer's Gang! pretty low characters in it!' They'd mean you, Huck. You wouldn't like that, and I wouldn't" (Mark Twain, *The Adventures of Tom Sawyer.*)

Adolescents sometimes are amusing, sometimes annoying, with their "we can't let you into the gang" exclusivism.

One "game" we grown-up Tom Sawyers go on playing is "We can't let you into the gang if you ain't respectable." We want a fellowship of the pure, the deserving—people like us. We screen out those who will not enhance our image, strengthen our viewpoint, bolster our pride, reinforce our prejudice, feed our egotism. Most country clubs, fraternities, and lodges—scrutinizing applicants to decide who is worthy of belonging—are examples of this childish game. So are the restrictive clauses or "gentleman's agreements" not to sell real estate to "undesirables" in certain residential neighborhoods.

This perverse side to human nature was (and still is) found even in

81

the church. One group, the "Hebrews," wanted to keep the fellowship restricted to "people just like us." This noisy, obstinate faction, claiming to be God's reconciling force, at the same time refused to be reconciled to others within their fellowship.

Within the church, the ultra-conservative's feelings were stiffening. Luke in the eleventh chapter of Acts reveals that this dissenting faction organized itself as "the circumcision party" (ACTS 11:2) and wielded immense influence.

Circumcision became the rallying point, the cause, the slogan for these dissident believers. In old Israel, the uncircumcised were believed to be alienated from God and corrupt. Up until this point, every man in the church—Apostles, Hellenist Jews, Samaritans—had been circumcised, the easily identifiable sign of the true believer.

The ultra-conservatives in the church noted the trend toward including "others" in their fellowship. They had stretched a point already in letting in the Samaritan Christians, but if this sort of thing were to continue, they reasoned, there was no telling who might come in. There had already been some disturbing talk by some of the hot-headed Hellenists such as Stephen and Saul about going to the Gentiles. It was time to take a stand, to stiffen the requirements for membership, the "Hebrews" felt. They knew that there was a quick, easy rule to keep "outsiders" out of the church: Were they circumcised? If not, that kept them away from God's promise, didn't it? Circumcision would be the fence that would keep out undesirables, *i.e.,* Gentiles, they reasoned.

Continuing such ancient practices in the church raised profound questions: Was the church to be an exclusive or inclusive fellowship? Was the gospel for all men or some? Does God have favorites? What are the qualifications for church membership?

Peter began his career as a sincere bigot. More interested in saving face than serving others he had to be pushed by Jesus into understanding that forgiveness meant seventy times seven. Even after the resurrection and Pentecost, his transformation was gradual. No cataclysmic event, as with Saul, abruptly and radically stretched Peter's horizons. Instead, starting with his tour of Samaria with John, a series of experiences slowly and painfully shifted Peter's thinking.

Peter, picking up the idea of itinerant preaching from such Hellenists as Philip, visited the congregations west of Jerusalem near the Mediterranean coast. Outside of Jerusalem again, the Spirit led Peter to do some unexpected things. First, he healed the paralytic Aeneas, one of the Greek-speaking former Jews at Lydda. Next, the

Spirit took Peter to Joppa where the congregation needed comfort following the death of a beloved member, Dorcas. In spite of the fact that Dorcas was a woman, Peter forgot his Old Testament scruples and acted as the Spirit's instrument to raise her. The Spirit pushed Peter past nearly all of his old boundaries, even sending him to stay at Joppa with an "unclean" man—one who handled dead animals, hence, was looked down on by strict Jews—Simon, a tanner. Almost without being aware of it, Peter began to break with old temple traditions.

Was Peter uneasy? Did his companions from Jerusalem comment on his behavior? Was Peter asking himself if this pattern would lead him to preach to Gentiles and perhaps even associate with them?

Peter needed something as drastic as a vision to drag him into contact with Gentiles. It was clearly not his idea to go to the despised Gentiles—it went completely against his upbringing and offended his deeply imbedded synagogue sensibilities.

Peter, in fact, was so much "old school" that he was strictly kosher when eating. One day when Peter was ravenously hungry in his chamber on the flat roof of Simon's house, the Spirit confronted him with the sight of a descending object which contained every kind of edible meat, "clean" and "unclean." The Spirit ordered Peter to eat, but Peter shrank from touching the "unclean." Up until that time, for Peter it was not just a minor infraction to eat "unclean" food; it was inherently wrong. Not once but three times, Peter turned down the Spirit's command.

Peter was bewildered about the meaning of this strange vision. While he was trying to interpret it, he was interrupted by visitors.

God sometimes answers our doubts and perplexities by sending others to us for help. The Spirit seldom packages neat bundles of answers for us—He is more likely to offer us opportunities to serve, and our questions begin to resolve themselves as we take up those opportunities. Interruptions are sometimes blessings.

Peter's interruption made possible the stretching of the horizons to include Gentiles in the church's fellowship. Following Peter's vision, the Spirit broke the last membership barrier in the early Christian community.

Peter's visitors were members of the staff of a company commander in the Roman Army named Cornelius. The name was that of a noble family of Rome, suggesting that Cornelius had distinguished ancestors. He probably groaned when his outfit, the Italian Cohort, was posted to Palestine. Boiling with revolt, Palestine spawned scores of guerrilla bands which specialized in picking off rising young Roman officers.

As part of the loathed occupation forces on a long tour of duty in the Middle East, Cornelius came into contact with Judaism and was deeply impressed. The man who embodied Rome's conquest of Israel later embodied Israel's conquest of Rome. Cornelius began to practice the Jewish customs of almsgiving and prayer and introduced these to his family and staff. As a commissioned officer, of course, he could never be circumcised or openly embrace Judaism.

What inner crisis was Cornelius going through? Why his spiritual restlessness? A prestigious family background, a secure position, a promising future—what more could any centurion ask for? Or did Cornelius sense the emptiness of all this, thinking as did another Roman soldier-seeker, "All is ephemeral—fame and the famous as well." (Marcus Aurelius, *Meditations* IV:35)

Posted to garrison duty at Caesarea, Cornelius had probably heard of "the Way." Possibly someone reported Philip's preaching, and the sensational news of Saul's radical new beginning no doubt had reached him. Perhaps he heard about Saul's hurrying through Caesarea to jump aboard a ship to escape his vengeful former associates. Did Cornelius long for the gift of first-hand apprehension of the Living God that these followers of the Galilean rabbi claimed that He brought?

In any case, Cornelius prayed. His prayer was answered when it was made clear that Peter was in the adjacent town of Joppa. A man used to making decisions, Cornelius immediately sent three of his staff to find Peter.

Acts indicates that it was more than coincidence that Peter experienced his vision the same day that Cornelius' men came to Joppa. With a fine sense of timing, the Spirit was preparing the stage for the first Gentile to be brought into the church. Cornelius' representatives interrupted Peter at the very moment he was puzzling over his dream.

Peter surprised himself by showing hospitality toward the three Gentile strangers. "He called them in to be his guests," (ACTS 10:23) a big step for a men who was raised to have deep scruples about defiling himself by eating with nonbelievers.

This was the day on which the Spirit stretched Peter's horizons. After hearing the strangers' report about Cornelius, Peter made arrangements to go the following day to Caesarea.

Cornelius' interest in the gospel was no private hobby. He had called together his family and friends to hear the Apostle. When Peter

84

and his party arrived, Cornelius, deeply respectful and grateful, prostrated himself before Peter in the presence of everyone.

A display of deference was customary in such circumstances but Peter briskly waved it aside, saying, "Stand up; I too am a man." (ACTS 10:26)

After this refreshingly honest greeting, Peter heard Cornelius' story, the account of a humble, devout man who was trying as hard as he knew to please God.

There are those in the church today who would have said to Cornelius, "Keep it up, Cornelius. As long as you are praying sincerely, giving conscientiously, and acting decently, you should be in good shape. I have nothing more to suggest."

Peter, however, did not tell Cornelius, "There is really nothing new or different to offer you. Besides, you'll be happier as you are." Instead, after sketching the Old Testament background, Peter swiftly moved on to the subject of Jesus Christ, climaxing his remarks with ". . . everyone who believes in him receives forgiveness of sins through his name." (ACTS 10:43)

The gospel is not one more recipe for "religion." God gives what man can never earn: forgiveness. No matter how sincere and sweaty the effort, man can never work hard enough at giving or praying or anything else to get himself right with God. God has done the impossible; He has come to man in the person of Jesus, establishing a new relationship.

"Everyone," Peter emphasized, "who believes in him receives forgiveness." It was completely unconditional. All who trust—whether Jew or Gentile—could receive new life through Jesus Christ!

The Holy Spirit completed what Peter was trying to verbalize. Luke writes that the ". . . Spirit fell on all who heard the word." (ACTS 10:44) The Spirit said Amen to Peter's statement, "Truly I perceive that God shows no partiality." (ACTS 10:34)

The "Gentile Pentecost" in Cornelius' house amazed those who had come with Peter. When Peter, wanting to welcome Cornelius and his gathering into the fellowship of the church, asked his six Jerusalem companions if they knew any obstacle to baptizing these Gentiles, they raised no objections. Whether the actual baptizing was done by Philip or one of Peter's party is unimportant (apparently it was not Peter); the significant fact is that at last the church of Jesus Christ understood the mission to be an inclusive fellowship. The Spirit finally demolished the last barrier. The first Gentiles were baptized.

Not only was Cornelius the first uncircumsised man to be baptized into the church, he was the first European. As the first Westerner to become a Christian, Cornelius is the spiritual ancestor of most of us. In addition, he symbolizes the pilgrimage of all of mankind: from pagan to Jew to Jesus; from Mars and deities of war to the Prince of Peace.

We may well hail the change in the church whereby Peter the prejudiced became Peter the pioneer. It was not easy, however, for Peter to return to his ultra-conservative Christian associates in Jerusalem. The news had flashed to Jerusalem ahead of Peter that he had repeatedly violated ceremonial law, even eating with "unclean" people, and worse, had smashed the never-to-be-broken taboo of welcoming Gentiles to the fellowship. Peter had already been regarded with suspicion after his Samaritan tour. This time, in Joppa and Caesarea, he seemed to have sold out altogether.

"The circumcision partly criticized him . . ." (ACTS 11:2). Literally this hostile, suspicious faction "separated" itself from Peter. It is one thing to disagree; it is another to give the cold shoulder.

Peter, however, had grown beyond his explosiveness of former days. Recounting the vision at Joppa, Peter patiently explained, ". . . the Spirit told me to go with them, making no distinction." (ACTS 11:12) Peter emphasized that it was not his doing, not some startling innovation which he concocted. Peter effectively silenced his critics. How could they argue against what Peter claimed that the Holy Spirit had done?

At the same time, Peter did not arrogantly claim to have a private hot line to the mind of God. Peter was not like the occasional crackpot we encounter who claims that he is "led by the Spirit," sometimes to do senseless, even appalling, things. Peter's own remarks indicate that he personally tested the Spirit's leading in two ways.

First, he did not act apart from the fellowship of other Christians. "These six brethren also accompanied me," Peter said, indicating that he refused to be a one-man church. Peter understood that the Spirit works with believers within the context of the church.

Second, Peter insisted upon checking always with what Jesus had said: "I remembered the word of the Lord, how he said, 'John baptized with water, but you shall be baptized with the Holy Spirit.' If then God gave the same gift to them as he gave to us when we believed in the Lord Jesus Christ, who was I that I could withstand God?" (ACTS 11:16-17) The Spirit interpreted Jesus and His words to Peter, and they became the authority for his mission to Cornelius.

The Scriptures are our "check" for the leading of the Spirit, as well. The eternal Word speaks through the words. We are not left to wonder whether or not it is really the Spirit prompting us on certain occasions—He gives us the Bible to test whether or not it is His leading. Unless confirmed in, by, and through Scripture, we can doubt that the "feelings" we all sometimes have are truly Spirit-inspired.

God's church or man's? The question is never completely resolved. Each generation of Christians, each congregation of believers is subtly tempted. Our experience is peculiarly similar to the first Christians: we want to erect barriers. We want to be choosy about those with whom we will associate.

In spite of our inclination to say NO to those not "our type," the Spirit keeps shouting Yes. ". . . *Everyone* who believes in him receives forgiveness. . . ." (ACTS 10:43) Forgiveness by Christ for everyone who believes means fellowship by us with everyone who believes!

12

THE CITY OF "FIRSTS"

(ACTS 11: 19-30)

IN THE FIRST CENTURY THE CITY OF ANTIOCH IN SYRIA, WITH AN estimated population of 600,000, was surpassed only by Alexandria and Rome itself. Nature was kind to Antioch—the Orontes River was navigable; the plain was fertile; the mountain scenery, picturesque. Antioch was rightly called "The Beautiful." Ancient travelers raved about its pleasant climate. The great network of Roman roads converged on this "Oriental Rome," emptying the mighty caravans from the East on its wharves and warehouses. Antioch boasted an outstanding university, encouraging art and literature enough to be lauded by Cicero, the great Roman orator, as a city of "most learned men and liberal studies."

But in spite of its reputation for business and culture, Antioch was known chiefly for its vice, corruption, and luxury. Oriental Greek cities were notorious—transplanting Athens and Rome to the Levant seemed to bring out the worst in both East and West. Antioch, a magnet for the vices of both Europe and Asia, was both the greatest and the worst city of the eastern Mediterranean world.

Gay, frivolous, dissolute, the people of Antioch lived for their pleasures. Life there was what one writer called "a perpetual festival of vice," revolving around the baths and the brothels, the amphitheater, and the circus. The notorious suburban pleasure garden of Daphne, ten miles in circumference, with its sanctuary of Apollo, fountains, cypress and laurel groves and colonnaded walks, encouraged every sort of immorality. Each year during the feast of Brumalia, lasting most of December, the entire city resembled a tavern, according to one contemporary. So much of Antioch's decadence and debauchery floated to Rome that the Roman satirist Juvenal quipped, "The Orontes empties into the Tiber." When Antioch wanted religion, it flocked to its host of magicians, charlatans, and miracle-workers. Babylonian astrologers found their most lucrative following in Antioch.

Eusebius, the ancient church historian, stated that Luke was a native of Antioch, although others think that he hailed from Macedonia. Regardless of whether Antioch was Luke's hometown, it holds a special place in his narrative. Antioch has three distinctions. It was the first great city to be confronted—and conquered—by the gospel. It was the place where believers in Jesus Christ were first called "Christians." And it was the place from which the church first sent aid to fellow Christians in another area, brothers who were probably unknown to most in the Antioch congregation.

Early believers did not hesitate to preach to those in blasé, brutal, and bustling Antioch, a radical departure. Previously, the gospel had been spread to the villages and small towns of Judea and Samaria, but with the appearance of a congregation in Antioch, the church moved out of the back channel into the main current.

Not everyone was comfortable with this latest innovation. The city of Antioch, to many in Jerusalem, was a corrupting environment. Its mixed population of Greeks, Syrians, Arabs, Romans, Jews, and what-have-you would never "take to" the gospel. Antioch was a complicated place, where the hustle and noise of commerce seemed to threaten the simplicity and purity of the faith. And Antioch's moral reputation? How could any sincere Christian in Jerusalem be certain that the standards of Apollo and Aphrodite would not infect the behavior of new Christians in Antioch?

Uneasy about the news of rapid growth in the congregation at Antioch, the "mother church" at Jerusalem decided to send someone to look into the matter and lend a hand. Peter, some thought, had proved to be wobbly. This time, they sent steady old Barnabas. Barnabas would not get carried away; he would keep these outsiders in line.

Barnabas was surprised and pleased by what the Spirit was doing in Antioch. He pitched into the work of evangelizing and helped bring "a large company" (ACTS 11:24) into the church. He quickly saw, however, that he needed help. Remembering his acquaintance from Tarsus named Saul whom he had befriended in Jerusalem a few years earlier, Barnabas went to Tarsus and searched intensively until he found him.

Barnabas deserves cheers for being the man who gave the church the Apostle Paul. Not only did he intercede for Saul at Jerusalem; Barnabas saw the value in having Saul minister among Gentiles. Barnabas must have realized that Saul with his superior energies and abilities would eventually eclipse him as number one leader, and he could have ignored Saul and stayed on at Antioch as head man in that congregation. But Jesus Christ, Barnabas knew, was to be first, and he was not afraid to be downgraded or demoted, even by a former enemy, if it meant upgrading and promoting Jesus.

Together in Antioch, Barnabas, Saul, and the city congregation were led by the Spirit to exciting and creative forms of ministry, and the church was never the same again. Using Antioch as a launching pad, the Spirit advanced the gospel into Asia Minor and Europe, leaping into cities throughout the Empire. No longer would the back-in-the-country Jerusalem mentality dominate the church. The Spirit determinedly led the church into Antioch, into The City, the place where decisions are made, tastes are created, standards are influenced.

The City is where people live—one out of eight Americans resides in great centers of a million-plus population. In 1850, only fifteen percent lived in cities; a century later, seventy percent. Soon, ninety-five percent of all new population in the U.S. will be urban dwellers.

The church is most truly in the Biblical tradition where it boldly stands in The City. Yet, in 1948, the Evangelism Report of the newly-formed World Council of Churches pinpointed three key areas in which the church had failed to penetrate: Islam, Hinduism—and "our great cities."

We can bring tears to our eyes with "There's a church in the valley by the wildwood." What if someone were to change the words of that old rouser to "There's a church in the ghetto by the stockyards!" The church—we—will not take The City seriously. To give only one example, during the twenty-five year period between 1940 and 1965, Presbyterians alone dissolved or merged thirty-three congregations in the city of Pittsburgh. No wonder the 173rd Presbyterian General Assembly with tongue in cheek remarked that the Protestant Church in The City "is marching fearlessly backward."

While the church has tried to get The City out of its hair, the Spirit insistently pushes the church back into Antiochs today. George Mac-Donald's verse says it well.

> I said, "Let me walk in the field."
> He said, "No, walk in the town."
> I said, "There are no flowers there."
> He said, "No flowers, but a crown."

Antioch, the city of "firsts" for the church, was also the place where "the disciples were for the first time called Christians." (ACTS 11:26) Strangely enough, the church at first resented the name. In the New Testament, believers dubbed themselves "disciples," "brothers," "saints," "the elect," but never "Christians." "Christian," in fact, is used in only two other places in the New Testament. In Acts 26:28, Agrippa sarcastically sneers at Paul, "In a short time you think to make me a Christian!" using the word contemptuously. In I Peter 4:16, Peter reveals that "Christian" was spoken by pagan persecutors with the same venom as "thief," or "murderer," and tells believers, "If one suffers as a Christian let him not be ashamed, but under that name let him glorify God."

Antioch people were well known for their mockery and sarcasm. Masters of ridicule, they lampooned actors and emperors alike. Emperor Julian, annoyed by their jibes at him, felt compelled to answer the Antioch public in writing. The punster who coined the slang term, "Christian," is nameless. Laughing Antioch took it up immediately as the best word to deride the party "Christus."

Antioch wondered, "Who are these peculiar people?" Some in Antioch probably heard Saul and Barnabas speaking of "the Kingdom" whose members were an "Army" under "the Christ." Calling them "Christians" was comparing them as an army to the "Pompeians," "Caesarians," and "Herodians." It was a great joke in Antioch to think of a crucified rabbi in the same terms as men of such power and prestige as Pompey, Caesar, and Herod. Originally, "Christian" was good for big laughs at Antioch.

Smarting under the reproach implicit in the name, believers in Antioch and elsewhere refused to use the title. Nonetheless, it quickly became the nickname by which the Roman world called followers of Jesus Christ. Tacitus (A.D. 116), writing of Nero's persecution about A.D. 64, referred to these "whom the populace called Christians." Pliny (A.D. 112), a Roman official nettled by the refusal of certain people to go along with emperor worship, wrote, "I asked them personally whether they were Christians; if they confessed it, I asked them a second and third time, threatening them with punishment. Then, if they adhered to their confession, I ordered them off to execution." To admit to being a "Christian" before a magistrate was tantamount to refusing to be part of the imperial cult.

Eventually, the word became a badge of honor. Just as the jeer of the Kaiser dismissing the British Expeditionary Force in 1914 as "that contemptible little army" led that dogged force to adopt the proud nickname, "The Old Contemptibles," so believers became

92

proud to be identified as "Christians." Eusebius describes Sanctus' trial in Gaul. When tortured by the authorities, Sanctus "steeled himself so firmly against them that he would not so much as tell his name or nation or city. All his answer to their inquiries was, 'I am a Christian.' "

There was an unintended compliment behind Antioch's contempt. "Christian" reveals what outsiders associated in their minds most with believers: Jesus Christ. Even Luke's Greek word for the disciples being *"called"* Christians emphasizes this. In Greek, the word meant originally "to transact business," but changed to refer to naming someone or taking a name from one's business. (This often happened in English family names, where, for example, such last names as Miller, Baker, Carpenter, Smith, Cooper (one who made barrels), Fletcher (one who made arrows), Weaver, or Sawyer came from the man's occupation.) "Christians" were occupied mostly with "Christus."

The suffix "-ian" at the conclusion of the word "Christ" meant that the Christ - ian was a "partisan of" Christ. Apparently these early believers impressed their foes with their devotion to Jesus Christ. These "partisans of Christ" rested their faith not on philosophy, not on theory, not on dogma, not on teaching, not on an institution, but on the Person of Jesus.

The nickname given—in both Greek and Latin—to Jesus' followers in the capital of Syria not only stuck, but signified the church's entrance into the vortex of the Roman world. From Antioch on, bearing the title "Christ's partisans," the church moved out of the parochialism of Jerusalem and out from the shadow of Judaism.

A story comes to us from the slave-running days of how a column of Africans in chains was being marched to a ship on the west coast of their native continent. One young man stood with immense dignity, head up and back erect, in spite of the manacles on his hands and feet, the bleeding welts on his back, in the midst of the moaning lines of miserable people. Pointing to this proud, unbent man in chains, someone commented, "He cannot forget that he bears the name of the chief."

Whether they used the name "Christian" or not, early believers could not forget that they bore the name of Jesus. The world had forced on them a new family name. A few generations later, glorying in the title, they incorporated in an ancient liturgy the prayer, "We thank Thee that the name of Thy Christ is named upon us, and so are we made one with Thee."

The congregation at Antioch was distinguished by another "first"; the sending of relief funds to distant fellow Christians in need.

During the Emperor Claudius' reign, there were periodic widespread food shortages. Tacitus, Suetonius, Dion Cassius, Josephus, Eusebius, and other ancient historians all testify to the distress caused by some of these famines, when food prices rose impossibly high and starvation was common.

Word reached the Antioch congregation of the need among believers nearly three weeks' journey away in Judea. Hardly anyone except Barnabas and Saul in Antioch had ever seen or met any from the church in Judea, and technically they were strangers. To the Antioch Christians, however, they were "brethren" (ACTS 11:29). In spite of geographical—and theological—differences, their common allegiance to Jesus Christ made them brothers, members of one family. The Antioch believers were the first with a world view of the church, the first with a sense of the unity among Christians, the first with responsibility toward distant, unknown members of the family of Christ's partisans.

The Antioch congregation sent money, ". . . every one, according to his ability. . . ." (ACTS 11:29) Remember that this congregation was undoubtedly made up of poor people—slaves, servants, laborers, commoners, people with precious little spare cash. Yet they shared!

These Antioch Christians sent more than money, vital though this was—they sent people. Expressing their personal concern toward Judean believers, they dispatched their best leaders, Barnabas and Saul. When they determined "to send *relief*" (ACTS 11:29), the word meant more than material aid. Relief also has to do with serving, with ministering. Important though dollars are, they take people to translate them into concern, to add the "plus" of love. Men without money cannot minister in action; money without men cannot act in ministry.

Serving by sending money and men! What better sign of life than this in any congregation? What better test for faith?

13

HOW CAN DICTATORS GET AWAY WITH MURDER?

(ACTS 12)

THE TRUCE WAS OVER. THERE HAD BEEN A BRIEF BREATHING SPACE after the persecution following Stephen's martyrdom blew itself out. This persecution had been directed mainly against Hellenistic Christians—Greek-speaking Jews-turned-Christian. The second, aimed at believers still in Jerusalem, caught the temple-going, Palestine-born, Aramaic-speaking "Hebrews," the disciples who had escaped the reprisals and arrests after Stephen's death.

The Jerusalem congregation, already hurting from the severe food shortages in Judea, was badly mangled by the sudden and furious attack by Herod. Two of the Apostles, members of Jesus' original group of The Twelve and key leaders in the young church, were seized. Following a lightning trial, James, son of Zebedee, was executed by being hacked to death—a cruel execution deliberately designed for this brave man to die in disgrace. Peter was kept in maximum security, waiting for the formalities of being sentenced to die.

The irony was that it was a political move by Herod, not an anti-church outburst. Although descended from the God-fearing Jewish Maccabees, the opportunistic Herod had been raised at Rome as a typical Roman playboy-adventurer. Between his wily nature and his good contacts in high places (especially with Emperors Caligula and Claudius), Herod moved himself ahead. Never popular with his own Jewish countrymen, he knew that he needed to mend his fences with the Jerusalem Establishment if he was going to stay on in Judea. Jailing two leaders of the obnoxious sect of followers of Jesus and killing one, Herod schemed, would delight the temple bigwigs. He cunningly planned to wring as much popularity as possible out of his persecution, contriving to terrify the riff-raff Christians by delaying Peter's trial and execution a few days. It was Passover time and people were pouring into Jerusalem, and crowd-pleaser Herod hoped to get more mileage out of Peter's death by having as many present as possible.

Joseph Conrad once wrote to a friend that life "made him feel like a cornered rat waiting to be clubbed." This seemed to be the outlook for the Jerusalem church. Why had James been executed? Why was Peter about to be? Why all this suffering? Why was Herod allowed to torture the church? What was the meaning in their loss and misery?

Haunted by the absurdity of life, suffering Christians must have asked where the Spirit was. Euripides' famous line was quoted frequently and believed widely: "The gods, too, whom mortals deem so wise are nothing clearer than some winged dream." Was the Holy Spirit a mere fantasy?

Herod's persecution must have been a time of severe testing for the Jerusalem congregation. Although there had been threats and alarms before, there had never been anything as vicious and determined as Herod's program to hamstring the church in Judea. Herod, not the Holy Spirit, seemed the chief actor in the world.

God acts—the early church believed this. As Chief Actor in the universe, He could be trusted. In spite of the injustice, the absurdity, the hopelessness of the church's situation, the Jerusalem believers did not think that God had given up. This beleaguered congregation, perhaps encouraged by the arrival of Barnabas and Saul, continued with what Luke called *"earnest* prayer" (ACTS 12:5). Luke uses the same word which described Jesus' prayer in Gethsemane, a wrestling with God, literally meaning "strained" or "stretched" to show its intensity.

There are no "explanations" about the enigma of suffering anywhere in Acts. The early church did not receive any "answers" to satisfy their questioning. There was the fact of tyranny and evil. Herod was real.

We usually best understand God's working during crises. The Bible is actually a record of turning points during which Israel learned to understand God's activities in the midst of history. The story of the church is a story of crises. It is incorrect to speak of the "development" of the Christian faith, as if it were a gradual growth or gentle, continual progress. Beginning with the catastrophic event of the cross, we understand God's plans through crisis: God was there, taking man's worst, and now we can be certain in any crisis that evil has been defeated. The greatest threat—that evil may overpower God—has been faced and vanquished.

The Spirit gave new understanding to the meaning of God's great act of deliverance at the cross by two lesser acts of deliverance for the Jerusalem church, the delivering of Peter from prison and the delivering of the Judean church from the clutches of Herod's tyranny. Luke gives the details of both of these exciting acts. To his readers, they were miraculous; to the church, they were new evidence of the Spirit's working.

Peter did not work himself loose. In fact, he did not have the faintest hope of going free. Herod had set Roman-style watches—four shifts, each lasting three hours—through the night. Two soldiers on each watch were chained to Peter and two more were posted outside his dungeon. With such maximum-security precautions, escape was impossible.

In spite of the discomfort and frequent disturbances, and in spite of the death sentence waiting the following day, Peter slept—and slept soundly, so soundly, in fact, that the God-sent messenger had trouble waking him!

To a society that spends $2,387,000 annually on sleeping pills and another $3,200,000 on tranquillizers, there is something striking in the phrase, ". . . Peter was sleeping between two soldiers . . ." (ACTS 12:6). In the midst of tension, a Christian can still lie down and receive the wonderful gift of a night's sleep. Put it another way: one who trusts God enough to let go and relax can lie quietly, knowing that whether he sleeps or wakes, whether he dies or lives, he rests on the Everlasting Arms of Him who "shall neither slumber nor sleep."

Peter was so bleary-eyed and groggy that he thought he was dreaming when he was told to dress, was taken past the snoring guards, was led through the dark passageways, and was turned loose on the street.

Precisely what happened? Again, Luke did not write to amuse us but to emphasize that the Spirit was still at work. In the midst of the horrors of Herod's holocaust, the Jerusalem church was reminded that the Spirit is stronger than security cells. As to details, Peter could only shake his head after that night and say, "Now I am sure that the Lord . . . rescued me from the hand of Herod. . . ." (ACTS 12:11)

Following the tension of James' death and Peter's near-death, Luke relates an amusing, almost comic-relief episode. Peter hurried through the sleeping city to the house of Mary, Barnabas' sister and John Mark's mother, apparently the headquarters for the believers in Jerusalem and perhaps the location of the Upper Room. Frantically beating on the heavy door at the gateway facing the street, Peter was anxious to get off the public thoroughfare before someone spread the alarm that he was missing. Inside Mary's house, many of the church were meeting to pray for Peter. A little servant girl named Rhoda heard Peter's knocking and timidly opened the gate a crack. She was so surprised to see Peter that she slammed shut the door, rushed into the prayer meeting and squealed hysterically that she had just seen Peter at the gate.

"You're crazy!" they snorted, (the literal meaning of "You are mad") (ACTS 12:15). Then hearing the pounding themselves, they succumbed to the strain of fatigue and worry and allowed themselves briefly to be pushed back to the level of superstitious folklore. "It is his angel!" they gasped. The banging continued. Pulling themselves together, they dashed to the door; sure enough, it was Peter. Waving his hands frantically to shush them, he slipped inside, closed the door, excitedly whispered what had happened, and instructed them to pass the word to James, Jesus' brother, one of the stalwarts in the Jerusalem congregation, and to the rest of "the brethren."

Luke cryptically adds, "Then he (Peter) departed and went to another place." (ACTS 12:17) Antioch? Caesarea? Samaria? Possibly any of these. Maybe even Rome. Perhaps Luke purposefully kept silent to protect sources or participants still living twenty years later.

Peter left town. Jerusalem officialdom was mystified. Peter had simply disappeared into thin air. Furious, Herod conducted a speedy court martial for the perplexed and terrified guards, pronounced the expected death penalty, and huffed off to Caesarea for a celebration to commemorate the birthday of Emperor Claudius.

There had been a long, ugly tiff between Herod and the city-states of Tyre and Sidon over duty payments. As Demosthenes said, "It is a rare matter for free cities to agree with monarchs," particularly true with greedy schemers like Herod. Never one to forget a grudge, Herod kept the pressure on the recalcitrant cities until they finally pleaded with his treasury official, Blastus, to intercede with Herod for an audience, which was set to coincide with the fete for the emperor.

It was a state occasion, a drama-packed moment, the pinnacle of triumph for Herod. Two powerful cities were forced to come crawling. Herod planned the details in order to savor every drop of victory. The celebration was to be held in the magnificent theater erected by Herod's grandfather, Herod the Great. Tier upon tier, cheering multitudes were to be gathered. The first day of the celebration, the necessary tip-of-the-hat to Claudius, was actually to be the build-up for Herod's Great Day.

The Jewish historian Josephus agrees entirely with Luke's details of Herod's dazzling entrance into the royal box at the Caesarea theater. Herod strutted in wearing lavish, gold-embroidered robes. The shimmering spectacle produced the expected cheers, with many of Herod's sycophants and favor-seekers saluting him as a Greek divinity. Instead of ignoring or refusing such empty adulation, Herod swelled pompously.

"Pride goes before destruction, and a haughty spirit before a fall," (PROVERBS 16:18) every Jewish boy learned by rote.

The cheering suddenly faded. Herod had collapsed. He was carried, dying, from the amphitheater. Luke, the medical man, later stayed at Caesarea for two years, probably collected eye-witness reports, and wrote down the concise cause of Herod's death: ". . . he was eaten by worms and died" (ACTS 12:23) or as the Greek has it, "he was as rotten as a worm-eaten tree." Not only was Herod's ending horribly painful, but it made him the laughing stock of the country, an ironic conclusion not only to Herod's celebration but to his career.

God sets limits to human evil. Even the most ruthless is ultimately called to account. "The more a man exalteth himself," Calvin observed, "the more doth he deserve to be cast down of God into the lowest hell with shame and reproach."

Herod, as was the case with all Napoleons and Hitlers, withered, decayed, and died. With a fine sense of the drama of contrasts Luke added immediately, "But the word of God grew and multiplied." (ACTS 12:24) The Spirit, as always, was the Doer, whose Acts climaxed Herod's acts.

"How does Herod get away with murder? Is God helpless?" the Judean church had wondered.

"The kings of the earth set themselves, and the rulers take counsel together, against the Lord and his anointed, saying, 'Let us burst their bonds asunder, and cast their cords from us.' He who sits in the heavens laughs; the Lord has them in derision." (PSALMS 2:2-3) God is still in charge of His universe, the church learned once again.

14

"WE TURN TO THE GENTILES"

(ACTS 13)

FEW NOTICE A HARDWOOD SAPLING IN THE WOODS. FOR A LONG TIME, it struggles in obscurity against fast-growing competitors, the sumacs and scrub pines which try to shoulder it into the shade. Finally there is a turning point, the decisive moment when that sapling succeeds in pushing through the ceiling of foliage hiding it. From then on, it begins its spread into a mighty tree, dominating the woods.

Like a hardwood sapling eventually topping its adversaries and unfurling into forest-top grandeur, so the church finally emerged from Palestinian obscurity and sang, bled, and prayed throughout the Roman Empire. The thirteenth chapter of Acts marks the turning point when the sapling church finally broke out of the shade of Judea to expand with restless power into world prominence.

Barnabas and Saul were back in Antioch after their Jerusalem visit, accompanied by Barnabas' young nephew, John Mark.

Barnabas and Saul were among the "prophets and teachers" at Antioch (ACTS 13:1). "Prophets and teachers" in this sense does not mean so much official assignments or offices as it means that Barnabas and Saul were making use of certain gifts from the Spirit. In the same list were Symeon called Niger, Lucius from Cyrene, and Manaen, one of Herod's staff (showing that the gospel had even penetrated the palace). These five formed the core of the committed.

"While they were worshipping the Lord and fasting, the Holy Spirit said. . . ." (ACTS 13:2) Note that the Spirit gave direction while they were worshipping and fasting. Significantly, the word for "worshipping" in Greek is the root for our English word "liturgy" and means *work*. Worship is work by the community of believers. It means that Barnabas, Symeon, Lucius, Manaen and Saul were struggling with Scripture, talking with each other, listening together, wrestling in prayer together. "Fasting" means more than simply doing without food. It implies a voluntary discipline. These "prophets and teachers" were like a group of well-trained skilled athletes straining together.

The church always needs a responsible remnant, a committed core. Only when a few are willing to use their gifts, struggle together with the Bible, and discipline themselves to listen in prayer, is the Spirit heard. The church is creative to the degree that a dedicated minority accepts the responsibility of worship and discipline.

The Antioch church did not accidentally stumble into the world mission or voluntarily whip up a burst of exuberance for preaching to outsiders. Undoubtedly Barnabas and Saul had heard in Jerusalem of Peter's tour of Joppa and Caesarea where the Spirit had led Peter to baptize Cornelius. Probably they reported this to the Antioch congregation. No congregation, however, is naturally enthusiastic about moving into the world to minister. The Agent who convinced the church at Antioch was the Spirit.

"Set apart for me Barnabas and Saul for the work to which I have called them," the Spirit instructed the Antioch church. (ACTS 13:2) The Greek word is the same as that used in the Septuagint (the Greek version of the Old Testament) translation of LEVITICUS 20:26 and NUMBERS 8:11, where certain ones are separated for service. This is the key to the meaning of ordination: certain persons are given specific functions.

Notice, however, that in "ordaining" Barnabas and Saul, the Antioch church simply sent them off to do a job. It did not elevate them to a new status or bestow on them a special grace or put them through a coronation ceremony to award them a lifetime title. Instead of conferring a standing for life—such as we usually associate with ordination—the early church at Antioch, handed Barnabas and Saul an assignment.

The ancient Jewish practice of laying hands on those being commissioned was observed, symbolizing that the entire church laid on Barnabas and Saul the task of mission. It meant in effect: "Barnabas and Saul, we the church recognize the unique talents the Holy Spirit has given you. We appoint you to go on behalf of all of us in the community of Christians. You do not go out as loners, nor as sole operators, nor as self-appointed revivalists. You are not embarking on a private tour. Rather, you represent all of us. We stand with you."

The word "Apostle" means "one who is sent." Apostolic succession really means being a "sending" church. In the early church, the essential meaning of ordination by laying on hands was sending out men for mission.

In spite of the mixture of backgrounds in its congregations and in spite of a rampant, debilitating paganism everywhere in the city, the church at Antioch was the Spirit's agent when it took the risk of sending out missionaries. In contrast to the timid, hesitant Jerusalem church, Antioch dared to be imaginative and bold. Perhaps the Jerusalem congregations were edgy after wholesale arrests and had to use their energies simply to survive. The initiative, in any case, passed to Antioch. Keen and eager to communicate the Good News, the Antioch church's action and ideas dominate Acts from chapter thirteen to the end.

The missionary church at Antioch sent Barnabas and Saul, later Silas and others, into Cyprus, then to the Turkish coast, then into the forbidding interior of Asia Minor, then across into Europe—everywhere! Luke gives us exciting glimpses of the mission church at work in the last half of his second volume.

With young John Mark "to assist them" (ACTS 13:5), Barnabas and Saul traveled the sixteen miles downstream to Seleucia, the port for Antioch, heading for the island of Cyprus. Using the proper nautical term, Luke tells us that the trio "sailed." (ACTS 13:4) (Luke's seaman's vocabulary is so technically correct that many scholars conjecture that he had been to sea himself or had lived in a port city.)

Cyprus' mountain tops are visible from the mainland on a clear day, and the island had a close tie with Antioch. A large colony of Jews had settled on Cyprus to work in the copper mines, enough to support several synagogues (see ACTS 13:5). Some of these who had heard of the gospel had helped set the Antioch church on its feet (ACTS 11:20). Barnabas himself hailed from Cyprus.

Landing at Salamis, Barnabas and Saul began an extensive evangelistic tour which took them to the opposite end of the island, one hundred miles away, to Paphos, the seat of Roman authority. The two most memorable men at Paphos were Sergius Paulus, the Roman proconsul, and Elymas Bar-Jesus, a fast-talking magician and turncoat Jew who styled himself a "prophet." The most notable event on Barnabas' and Saul's missionary tour of Cyprus was their encounter with these two.

Although subtly pointing out to his readers (including Theophilus, the man for whom Acts was written) that Roman officials were open to the gospel and not necessarily implacable enemies, Luke did not disguise the fact that Sergius Paulus dabbled in occult matters and enjoyed being entertained by Elymas Bar-Jesus. Even the most sophisticated and educated Romans consulted oracles, believed in astrology, and took sorcerers seriously. The Emperor Tiberius kept a flock of Eastern wizards around him. The historian Tacitus, commenting on his Roman fellow citizens' nervous preoccupation with astrologers, wrote that these fakes "will always be discarded and always cherished."

Elymas Bar-Jesus shrewdly saw that he would be out of a job if Sergius Paulus took Barnabas and Saul seriously. Trying to sway his benefactor, Elymas Bar-Jesus superciliously tried to discredit the gospel.

Saul saw that he would have to deal with this troublemaker immediately before they could do anything. Meeting Elymas head-on, Saul nailed him as the imposter and corrupter which he was. "Bar-Jesus" means literally "son of salvation." With a play on words on Elymas Bar-Jesus' name, Saul denounced him as "son of the devil." As if this fierce tongue lashing were not enough, Saul—perhaps thinking of his own Damascus Road experience—predicted that Elymas would also be struck blind for a time so that he could awaken to the reality of the Risen Jesus Christ.

Luke's medical terms in ACTS 13:11 imply that Elymas' sight began to wane as he went through the stages of developing cataracts. Luke's point, however, is that Jesus Christ is stronger than the wiles of any hocus-pocus artist.

Elymas Bar-Jesus' blindness opened the eyes of Sergius Paulus. The episode also altered the missionary team in two ways. First, Saul emerged as the leader of the party. Formerly, the travelers had been referred to as "Barnabas and Saul" and at the beginning of Chapter Thirteen, the list of five "prophets and teachers" put Saul's name last. In ACTS 13:13, the threesome of Barnabas, John Mark, and Saul is abruptly labelled "Paul and his company," and from this point on in Acts Paul's name almost always appears first.

The second big change in the missionary trio was that Saul took a new name. In ACTS 13:9, Luke writes, "But Saul, who is also called Paul . . ." and subsequently always refers to him as Paul.

Was Saul, to use the new word in vogue among foreign missionaries, trying to "indigenize," trying to identify as much as possible with non-Jews? "Paul" is a Roman name. Saul, realizing that his mission lay in working with Gentiles as well as Jews, might have deliberately chosen to go by a Gentile name. Again, Saul's encounter with Sergius Paulus and Elymas Bar-Jesus had been a victory, and in the Hebrew tradition great victories were sometimes celebrated by taking new names, as when Abram became Abraham, Jacob became Israel, Simon became Peter. The change from Saul to Paul signified a victory among Gentiles, and signalled a shift in the Spirit's activity.

From Cyprus, Paul, Barnabas and young John Mark took a ship to the southern coast of Asia Minor, landing at the city of Perga in the district of Pamphylia. Perhaps originally they merely planned to survey the area before returning later to plant congregations. In contrast to Cyprus, which was always described as "Happy" or "Blessed," Perga was steaming and sickening, its climate so miserably hot in the summer that most of its population fled to the mountains. Perga, located on a mosquito-ridden plain, was a malarial hole.

The visit to Perga was the beginning of what Paul later referred to as his "thorn" (II CORINTHIANS 12:7), undoubtedly a severe attack of malaria. "You know it was because of a bodily ailment that I preached the gospel to you at first" (GALATIANS 4:13), Paul wrote, adding that he was so ill that his "condition was a trial" (GALATIANS 4:14) when in Perga and Galatia. Alternating between searing temperatures—sometimes up to 106 degrees—occasionally ending in delirium and death, and severe chills—the "shakes" where a man in the stifling tropics pleads for more blankets to warm his shivering body—malaria racks a patient without drugs for weeks on end. Once in a person's bloodstream, it recurs suddenly in the years after the initial attack. Without aralin, atabrine, or modern medicines, Paul would have been incredibly weak.

A second set-back hit Paul. John Mark insisted on deserting the party and returning to his home in Jerusalem. Perhaps Mark was homesick, tired, and frightened. Perhaps he was anxious about conditions back in famine-stricken Jerusalem, and concerned about his widowed mother. Perhaps he was uneasy that he was getting in deeper than he had bargained for. The prospect of staying in Asia Minor was not inviting, especially if the party moved into the wild, bandit-infested, mountainous interior. Possibly Mark was uncomfortable about associating with Gentiles so much, or he may have been somewhat miffed because his uncle, Barnabas, was no longer in charge of the group. Mark, who had not been commissioned by the church at Antioch, felt no responsibility to remain. Abruptly, he left Paul and Barnabas, to the former's annoyance and disappointment.

Scholars have never come up with a sensible answer as to why Paul and Barnabas left Perga to go into the interior. Admittedly Perga was unhealthy and somewhat deserted, but why did they not catch a ship to Antioch, or even back to Cyprus? The only answer is the obvious one: they were determined to leave a trail of congregations before returning home. Feverish and wobbly though Paul was, he refused to quit.

The journey on foot through the Pisidian highlands was physically rigorous enough to give pause to the hardiest. The trails clung to huge cliffs and slanted up to dizzying heights. Two of the most treacherous rivers in the world had to be forded, the Cestrus and the Eurymedon, violent, enormous cascades boiling down steep, narrow ravines. The really frightening part of the trip, however, was the threat of death from the hordes of cut-throats who swept down from mountain lairs on travelers. Even Alexander the Great, with his mighty army, had unexpectedly found that the toughest part of his campaign to join Parmenio in Phrygia was shaking off the forays of the brutal, lawless tribesmen in the Taurus mountains.

Paul and Barnabas probably joined one of the caravans going through the passes. Travelers did this for protection, much as later travelers joined wagon trains before the American West was settled. Even so, it was a journey that Paul remembered the rest of his life, and probably had in mind when he reminisced how he had been ". . . in danger from rivers, danger from robbers . . . danger in the wilderness . . . in toil and hardship, through many a sleepless night, in hunger and thirst, often without food, in cold and exposure." (II CORINTHIANS 11:26-27)

Across the mountains bordering the coast of what today is southern Turkey is a high, bleak table-land; in Paul's day, this was an inhospitable plateau filled with dreary towns whose natives spoke a Pisidian dialect.

A sizeable Jewish population had settled in Asia Minor, and nearly every city had enough people to maintain a synagogue. For Paul and Barnabas, the pattern was invariably the same: to the synagogue first. Why to the synagogue, especially when the opposition became so bitter that a fierce reaction nearly always follows? First, the synagogue provided a ready-made audience. Second, it offered the most receptive group, the best soil for initial efforts. Partially prepared prospects, the synagogue-goers were people who already had had some grounding in the Old Testament. Paul and Barnabas felt some sense of obligation to go to their own people first.

Once in Antioch, the leading city of Pisidia (not to be confused with Antioch in Syria, home base for Paul and Barnabas), the pair of missionaries entered the local synagogue as strangers, probably putting on their prayer shawls, the badge identifying themselves as Israelites. They listened to the reading of the first and second lessons, selections from the law and the prophets. It was customary after the readings for the head of a synagogue to invite newcomers or visitors to address the congregation to give any "word of consolation" or encouragement.

Luke gives us a summary of Paul's preaching in ACTS 13:17-41 by quoting large sections of his sermon at Antioch of Pisidia. Although Paul preached hundreds of times, this is one of the few samples of his sermons to be passed on to us.

The most obvious thing about Paul's sermon is its striking similarity to both Peter's and Stephen's. There is a fundamental agreement on the basic personal experience of knowing Jesus Christ: God offers forgiveness, release, freedom, and new life through Jesus Christ. The central theme in every sermon presented in Acts is what God has done through the cross and resurrection.

At the same time, Paul injects distinctive, personal touches of his own. "Let it be known to you, therefore, brethren, that through this man forgiveness of sins is proclaimed to you, and that by him everyone that believes is freed from everything from which you could not be freed by the law of Moses." (ACTS 13:38-39) Other preachers had hinted at what Paul spells out clearly here. Paul states what came to be called the doctrine of justification by faith, and the church's understanding of the universality of the offer of forgiveness.

"Justification by faith" means that we cannot get ourselves right with God by what *we* do. All of our efforts to justify ourselves or appear "good" by keeping rules are doomed to failure. Paul, knowing what it is to be trapped in guilt and hopelessness by trying to be legally proper, tells us that only by our trust in God, who has broken into our lives in the cross and resurrection, can we be saved.

Paul used a warm, affectionate tone with his own people as he pleaded with them, addressing them as "Brethren, sons of the family of Abraham. . . ." (ACTS 13:26) Forget trying to save yourself by your own efforts to keep the law, he urged.

At the same time, Paul made it clear that God's deliverance in Jesus Christ is for all men. While many in the audience were thrilled and excitedly asked for more, other listeners caught the implications of his reference to forgiveness for *"everyone* that believes." (ACTS 13:19) Later, outside the synagogue, they cross-examined Paul and Barnabas. Did Paul mean what he said about *everyone* being offered forgiveness of sins?

During succeeding days the following week, Paul's sermon was widely discussed. By the following Sabbath, the lines were drawn. The synagogue was packed. This time, Paul received a mixed reaction. While some were attracted, the leaders were indignant, resentful that outsiders should be admitted to what they considered to be their exclusive heritage of salvation. Paul, they shouted, was all wrong. It was unfair, they claimed, to have him selling out his background.

As the synagogue leaders roared their disapproval and shouted down Paul and Barnabas, the two missionaries made a momentous decision. Filled with a deep sense of urgency, they replied to the angry synagogue crowd, "It was necessary that the word of God should be spoken first to you. Since you thrust it from you, and judge yourselves unworthy of eternal life, we turn to the Gentiles." (ACTS 13:46) If these hearers did not want the good news, then on to others!

To the Gentiles! To strict Jews, Gentiles were dogs, and "dogs" did not mean friendly household pets but snarling, evil street scavengers, running in ferocious packs, hated and feared in the villages. What a momentous change in the direction of the church! Gentiles as well as Jews were to be presented the gospel on equal terms! How grateful we should be! Had it not been for this decision by Paul and Barnabas, there is a strong possibility that we would be Gentile outsiders with no knowledge of Jesus Christ.

Paul and Barnabas were not stomping off in a huff, petulantly pouting. Their mission to the Gentiles was not rancor or disappointment with the Jews but a deepened awareness of the Bible's message. "I have set you," Paul and Barnabas remembered Isaiah's words, "to be a light for the Gentiles." (ISAIAH 49:6 quoted in ACTS 13:47) The real mission of Israel, the church recalled, was to present the Lord to outsiders.

In spite of the fact that his thrust was to the Gentiles after his visit to Pisidian Antioch, Paul did not ever think of himself as any less a Jew, nor did he ever cease trying to win fellow Jews. To the end of his life, Paul carried the rejection of Jesus as lord and Saviour by the Jews as a personal sorrow and a matter of deep concern. In fact, his last recorded interviews in Acts were with leaders of the synagogue at Rome.

15

TALE OF FOUR CITIES

(ACTS 14)

THE SYNAGOGUE SCENE AT PISIDIAN ANTIOCH WAS ONLY A CURTAIN-raiser for what followed on Paul's first missionary journey—and for the rest of his life.

Antioch of Pisidia, headquarters for a Roman administrative district, was supposed to have some big-city sophistication. Nevertheless, its community leaders were egged on to be suspicious of Paul and Barnabas, and just when the outlook for the church began to look promising, Paul and Barnabas were driven out of the district.

Instead of heading home, the intrepid pair stormed the next city, Iconium. Formerly a frontier town, Iconium was officially constituted as a Roman colony by the Emperor Hadrian. Its population was the usual conglomeration of ex-soldiers, expatriate Jews, Roman government officials, Syrian merchants, and half-civilized excitable natives.

Paul and Barnabas stayed in Iconium "for a long time" (ACTS 14:3). It was, however, the same story as at Antioch, except that Iconium was less sophisticated. The accusations against Paul and Barnabas finally hardened into a threatened charge of blasphemy, punishable by death by stoning, and Paul and Barnabas were forced to flee for their lives.

All that Paul and Barnabas had apparently succeeded in accomplishing since landing in Asia Minor was to win the title "Apostle," previously only carried by the Twelve. In ACTS 14:4, at Iconium, Luke dubs Paul and Barnabas "Apostles" for the first time.

But Paul and Barnabas were Apostles on the run. Farther and farther they advanced into remote Asia Minor. Iconium was the hub of the sheep-raising district. Other centers were nothing more than dusty provincial market towns in the barren, windswept hinterland. The greater the distance from Perga on the coast, the greater the dangers. Opposition from synagogues, from crooked magistrates, from superstitious natives, from hostile magician-astrologer-priests, all slowed down the Apostles' evangelism program.

The Arctic explorer, Alexander Mackenzie, hoping to find an opening to the Pacific Ocean, followed a great river in northern Canada for weeks, expecting to have it bring him to his goal. Instead, it finally landed him on the icy shores of the Arctic Ocean. Discouraged and frustrated, Mackenzie named it "River of Disappointment."

Life, in spite of its pattern of rejections and setbacks in Asia Minor, was no river of disappointment to Paul and Barnabas. Although they were meeting people more and more boorish and brutal, they did not complain how it was useless to preach in the boondocks. They were at the end of the Roman highway by the time they reached Lystra; Paul and Barnabas, however, did not look upon it as a blind alley.

The town of Lystra, boisterous and backward, lay six hours' hard walk south southwest from Iconium. Although the people of Lystra could understand Greek well enough to catch what Paul and Barnabas were saying, they preferred their own primitive Lycoanian language. The local religion was a blend of folk superstitions. Most accepted the tale that Jupiter and Mercury had once, incognito, visited the neighboring area, and hundreds made pilgrimages to the alleged site of the gods' personal visitation.

Since there was no synagogue at Lystra, Paul and Barnabas searched out the next likeliest place to find an audience—the marketplace. They quickly noticed a sight familiar to any Eastern town, a cripple hunched on the street. Observing that the cripple was listening intently, Paul suddenly interrupted his address and shouted, "Stand upright on your feet." (ACTS 14:10)

To the astonishment of everyone who knew that he had been a cripple from birth, who had never stood on his feet, the man sprang up and walked!

The marketplace crowd of shoppers, loafers, bypassers, storekeepers went wild. Never had anything like this been seen. Joyous, shouting people surged around Paul and Barnabas, babbling in Lycoanian.

Paul and Barnabas did not discover until much later what all the excitement was about. Someone finally explained to them that the town thought that Paul and Barnabas were the gods Hermes and Zeus, making a personal appearance. To their horror, Paul and Barnabas further discovered that plans were swiftly shaping up to hold a great ceremony honoring them as deities!

Zeus, the chief of the ancient Greek pantheon, and Hermes, his eloquent, popular lieutenant—the great, benign Barnabas and busy, talkative Paul fitted the patterns beautifully. Greek writer Ovid passes on some of the many folktales of gods walking on earth and historians verify how gullible the back-country people were.

A holiday-spirit hooked the Lystra citizenry. Sacrificial bulls were paraded; fires were prepared. Giddy crowds surged through the streets waiting for the festival to begin.

Shocked that they were unwittingly being party to a wild, pagan spree, Paul and Barnabas rushed back to the marketplace, tearing their clothes to show their anguish and crying, "Men, why are you doing this? We also are men, of like nature with you. . . ." (ACTS 14:15)

Nobody likes to be made to look silly. Paul's speech made the people of Lystra feel like fools. He had disillusioned them about a visit of gods and had spoiled their party.

Disillusioned people grow sour and sullen, and usually take out their resentments on the one who spoils their illusions. It still does not take much to incite a riot in primitive parts of the world, and it took very little to stir the sullen Lystra marketplace into a lynch mob. Some skilled rabble-rousers from the Antioch synagogue one hundred thirty miles away, determined to wreck Paul and Barnabas' efforts, whipped the Lystra crowds into a fury. Shouts of rage . . . pounding feet . . . dust . . . flying stones . . . shrieks . . . the animal roar of a mindless mob out for blood. When it subsided, a human body was left, abandoned, presumed dead, on the dump outside the town.

Although he was not mentioned in Luke's narrative, one witness to the day's grisly events was a shy, sensitive young man, Timothy, son and grandson of two devout Jewish women, Lois and Eunice. Although helpless to stop the outrage against Paul, these three were certainly among the "disciples gathered about him" (ACTS 14:20) after the crowd went home. Later Timothy, a trusted helper, was to receive two of Paul's most personal letters, and was referred to as a "son" by Paul.

Miraculously, Paul was not seriously injured. The believers at Lystra bandaged, nursed, and nourished Paul that night and speeded him and Barnabas on their way before daybreak. They promptly headed for the next town, dreary Derbe, on a side road, the last possible place they could have visited without retracing their steps to Iconium.

How could they keep going, especially Paul, after being brutally cut and bruised by the stoning mob, after tension-packed weeks of trying to speak and being expelled in a series of towns, after a grueling climb through the mountain gorges, after a debilitating bout of malaria?

". . . I have learned, in whatever state I am, to be content," writes Paul in Philippians. "I know how to be abased, and I know how to abound; in any and all circumstances I have learned the secret of facing plenty and hunger, abundance and want. I can do all things in him who strengthens me." (PHIL. 4:11-14)

"I can do all things" . . . even drag a battered, bleeding body through a hostile countryside to Derbe. Derbe was the only city on the first missionary journey in Asia Minor in which Paul and Barnabas did not provoke a riot. They, for once, ". . . preached the gospel to that city and had made many disciples. . . ." (ACTS 14:21)

When it was time to return home, it meant retracing their steps through Lystra, Iconium, and Antioch. There was no other route. Paul and Barnabas knew they were risking pain, even death, to return to any of these cities; they were re-entering the lion's cage to go near Lystra. They not only did so, but they deliberately stopped off in each place to train and strengthen converts and organize the tiny, new congregations.

There is a risk in being a Christian. Eleven Baptist missionaries in the Philippines in 1941 also knew this. Although they could have escaped at the time of the Japanese invasion, they risked torture and death by deciding to remain with their churches, ministering and witnessing. Their risk ultimately meant arrest, and, days before the American liberation in 1945, beheading.

God, however, risked everything at the cross, on the darkest day the world has ever known. And God won! He turned a crucifixion into a resurrection.

Our tiny risks now mean nothing. Even though we may bleed or even die, we can risk even life itself for the gospel with the triumphant certainty that the biggest risk has already been taken. God is victorious. He can be trusted to handle *anything*.

As Paul and Barnabas retraced their painful journey, stopping off in each town as unobtrusively as possible, Luke tells us that they ". . . appointed elders for them in every church. . . ." (ACTS 14:23) In other words, they set up an organizational framework within each congregation.

Although Paul and Barnabas probably hoped to return someday to the congregations at Lystra, Iconium, and Antioch of Pisidia, they knew it might be years or even never, and that they might not only face stones, but possible defeat. Would these new Christians be willing to pay the price of non-conformity? Would the untried leaders of these infant churches be able to keep them alive?

Luke states simply that Paul and Barnabas ". . . committed them to the Lord in whom they believed." (ACTS 14:23) "Committed" is a banking term, which means entrusting valuables or leaving money in a bank. Paul and Barnabas deposited their new converts with the Lord for safe keeping. With such trust, Paul and Barnabas could march homeward with optimism.

There was a stopover in Perga after descending the mountain passes, where the hot season had passed and the population had returned. After preaching in Perga, Paul and Barnabas hiked the sixteen miles to Attalia and took a ship for home.

Testimonial banquets and glowing citations for the two returning missionaries? Never! Not one word of personal credit! "And when they arrived, they gathered the church together and declared all that God had done with them and how he had opened a door of faith to the Gentiles." (ACTS 14:27) Not what Paul and Barnabas had done, but "all that *God* had done, "how *he* had opened a door of faith to the Gentiles." Amazing though their accomplishments were, the two new Apostles refused all personal acclamations. Their motto could have been that of the Reformers, *"Sola gloria Dei,"* TO GOD ALONE BE ALL THE GLORY!

16

CONTROVERSY AND THE COUNCIL

(ACTS 15: 1-35)

THE DIFFERENCES BETWEEN THE "HELLENISTS" AND THE "HE-brews" had never been resolved. Hesitant and perplexed at the idea of including uncircumcised outsiders, the conservative synagogue group reluctantly accepted such non-Jews as the Ethiopian (ACTS 8) and Cornelius (ACTS 10), and even these were welcomed only as the result of a special revelation. The circumcision party consoled itself with thinking that these were "exceptional cases."

It was a very different matter to hunt out Gentiles and take them in wholesale, welcoming them as equals. It seemed unfair to rank ex-pagans as co-inheritors of the covenant with those who had scrupu-lously kept all the synagogue rules, and many in the church resented being asked to do so.

Furthermore, the influx of Gentiles into the church was threatening to the circumcision party. If the present trend continued, it reasoned, all the old standards of conduct would change. "Relax the rules on circumcision and eating, and where do you stop?" these churchmen asked, murmuring that such unchecked waiving of the old Jewish practices would result in libertarianism.

Antioch, the Christian capital of the north, quickly adopted the habit of substituting baptism for circumcision as the initiation cere-mony to the fellowship. When Paul and Barnabas made their phe-nomenally successful missionary tour of Cyprus and the cities of southern Asia Minor, droves of uncircumcised were brought into the church.

To the ultra-conservatives in the circumcision party, the time had come to take a stand. Paul's radical activities were undermining the cherished traditions of the fathers and the very future of the faith was at stake.

Without the backing of James or any of the other Jerusalem church leaders, certain of these self-appointed guardians of the faith sent a "truth squad" to Antioch and over Paul's route in southern Asia Minor. "Unless you are circumcised according to the custom of Moses, you cannot be saved," (ACTS 15:1) they insisted. Worse, the circumcision clique stirred up intrigues against Paul and Barnabas.

". . . Paul and Barnabas had no small dissension and debate with them . . ." (ACTS 15:2), and Luke's words in the Greek reveal how deep the discord ran.

The one good thing in all this was that it forced the young church to make up its mind on the crucial question: Is a man saved by grace or by keeping rules? Was what was done through the cross and resurrection enough or not? "Unless you are circumcised . . ." maintained the Judaizers, "you cannot be saved." "Unless you believe in Jesus Christ," insisted Paul's party, "you cannot be saved." What *was* the norm for salvation?

The Council of Jerusalem which finally resolved the circumcision controversy was a decisive event in world events, for later world history would have been drastically different had the circumcision party prevailed. The Jerusalem Council was the show-down on whether or not the gospel would be allowed to stand untouched by the church. If those who were determined to improve on the gospel by forcing circumcision on all converts had had their way, the church would have retreated back to Judaism instead of moving forward with Jesus Christ.

After the discussions at Antioch between Paul's party and the circumcision party ended in deadlock, it was agreed to present the matter to the Jerusalem "mother" church. The Antioch congregations appointed Paul, Barnabas, and some of the others to be their spokesmen. One of "the others," Paul tells us in Galatians 2, was Titus, a devout and respected believer who had never been circumcised. According to Galatians 2, Titus became a sort of "test case," the principle under discussion centering specifically on him. As the Antioch delegation traveled south, their trip turned into something of a triumphal tour. Congregations in Phoenicia and Samaria heard the reports gladly and were enthusiastic about Paul's work. The atmosphere in Jerusalem, however, was chilling. The bigoted, bitter "party of the Pharisees," (ACTS 15:5) the angriest of the circumcision party, jumped up, denouncing Paul's procedures and attacking the doctrine of grace.

Luke did not keep the minutes of the meetings that followed, but simply passed on the highlights of the entire assembly. Obviously there were also many private, unrecorded conferences. Piecing together Luke's brief journal in Acts 15 and Paul's account in Galatians 2, the sequence was something as follows: First, a stormy, public meeting at which the party of the Pharisees rose up, and said, "It is necessary to circumcise them, and to charge them to keep the law of Moses." (ACTS 15:5) Next, relying on Galatians 2, a series of private meetings and informal conversations followed over a period of several days. Finally, a second meeting of the entire assembly was called. At this, the first full-scale Church Council, Luke says, "The apostles and the elders were gathered together to consider this matter." (ACTS 15:6)

James, not Peter, was the presiding officer. Preeminent among the apostles, James was deferred to by all parties as the most esteemed and his handling of the council reflects his nickname, "the Just."

Peter, of course, was listened to as one carrying great weight. Luke reported the gist of Peter's speech, the last recorded words of Peter in Acts. Remarkably similar to both Paul's and John's themes, Peter's argument was a summary of the theology of the early church.

Referring to his own mission to the Gentiles at Caesarea when Cornelius was baptized some ten or twelve years earlier, Peter reminded everyone that the Spirit was given to these uncircumcised brethren as much as to those raised in the traditions of Moses. Then, echoing Paul's words in Galatians 5:1, Peter slashed to the heart of the controversy: circumcision and other Mosaic requirements have been made into a yoke on the necks of new believers. "Now therefore why," demanded Peter, "do you make trial of God by putting a yoke upon the neck of the disciples which neither our fathers nor we have been able to bear?" (ACTS 15:10)

Rising to a ringing climax, Peter concluded with words which became the theme of the council. In contrast to the externals emphasized by the circumcision party, Peter proclaimed, ". . . We shall be saved through the grace of the Lord Jesus, just as they will." (ACTS 15:11)

After this stirring address, the crowd was silent. Paul and Barnabas took the floor. Wisely, they gave no rousing speeches; instead, they quietly ". . . related what signs and wonders God had done through them among the Gentiles." (ACTS 15:12) The emphasis was on what God had done, not Paul or Barnabas.

Summing up the argument advanced by Peter, James not only agreed but found support for the position in the Scriptures. The Old Testament writers promised a new Kingdom of the line of David, and in Jesus, this promise was fulfilled. Pentecost was the restoration of

117

the Kingdom. According to God's original intention, Gentiles were meant to be called to the Kingdom—the prophets, James said, attested to this. Reciting relevant passages from Amos 9:11-12, Jeremiah 12:15 and Isaiah 45:21, James, although Hebrew to the core, quoted the Greek version of the prophets, undergirding his understanding that Gentiles were to be included in Christ's church.

James was only chairman of the council. He merely voiced the consensus of the delegates, rather than making an *ex cathedra* pronouncement. His words, therefore, reflect the corporate mind of the council.

"My judgment," James announced, "is that we should not trouble those of the Gentiles who turn to God. . . ." (ACTS 15:19) James' decree completely vindicated Paul. More important, it was a triumph of God's concerns over the institution's interests, a victory of God's inclusivism over man's exclusivism.

The second part of James' decree was a request for satisfactory personal behavior by Gentile believers. The conduct of the average non-Christian in those times was scandalous, and many new converts carried their old habits with them into the church. James warned all new converts to avoid any tinges of pagan culture, not to placate the Jews or to keep from offending their sensibilities, but rather, to make a clean break with the past.

Specifically, James enjoins Gentile converts to stay clear of three things: ". . . to abstain from the pollutions of idols and from unchastity and from what is strangled and from blood." (ACTS 15:20)

Some mistakenly assert that James merely laid a new set of rules, another "yoke," on the necks of Gentile believers. Rather, James sensibly pointed out the dangers and responsibilities of being a believer.

The feasts and orgies in heathen temples in most cities were warp and woof of the Roman way of life. Telling new converts "to abstain from the pollutions to the idols" was James' way of counseling them to avoid pagan rituals. James also warned Gentiles to guard themselves against the enticements of the loose moral practices so prevalent in the Roman world.

To avoid meat from strangled or unbled animals may seem to us to be a silly superstition or a throw-back to the Levitical code (LEVITICUS 17:13; DEUTERONOMY 12:16, 23). Blood, to the ancients, however, was life. Out of a compassion for life, the Jews would not eat or drink blood. James wanted all Christians to have a reverence for life.

Hacking a road across the Alleghenies, British General John Forbes moved against the French and occupied Fort Duquesne on November 27, 1758. Few at that time saw any great significance in the fact that a company of hungry Highlanders had captured a remote French outpost in the wilderness. Astute scholars such as Woodrow Wilson, however, have pointed out that this event was a turning point in history because it meant the end of French domination in much of North America. The French king had been trying to impose old France in the New World. A different language, a different form of government, a different legal system, a different culture, even a different religion would have resulted. The Forbes Road and capture of Fort Duquesne meant that the English language, form of government, and culture were stamped on our nation. More important, the road was open at newly-named Fort Pitt for a practical and safe entrance to the West, through which pioneers poured.

The Jerusalem Council was likewise a decisive turning point in the history of the Church. The Council meant a show-down between restrictive rules and liberating Love. The church agreed to give us the exhilarating freedom and awesome responsibility of relying completely on the grace of Jesus Christ.

The council also settled the question of whether or not the church would reach out to *all* men. Christians agreed finally that to take seriously their missionary task, ratifying the Great Commission, "Go therefore and make disciples of all nations. . . ." (MATTHEW 28:19)

The council also had something to say about the thorny question of controversy within the church. Obviously, there was disagreement in the early church— even the experience of the Holy Spirit did not guarantee that there would be absence of conflict. There was dissension even among those men, many of whom had known Jesus personally, all of whom had been rebaptized by the Holy Spirit. They were human; they were subject to error; they were opinionated. Each side was convinced the other was corrupting the faith, and that the church would take a radically different course if the other faction had its way. Yet in spite of tension and tempers, the church sensed its unity in Jesus Christ through the Holy Spirit.

Unfortunately, the modern church has only begun to learn the lesson from the circumcision controversy. Too often, we extend our dislike of our Christian brother's argument to a dislike of the brother himself. Even the peace-loving members of the Society of Friends once disagreed so vehemently during a Meeting at which followers of Quaker Elias Hicks were expounding their views in 1828 in Philadelphia that a fist fight erupted and the Quakers were split into rival Meetings on Arch Street and Race Street!

At Jerusalem, the Spirit bestowed upon Christians the art of disagreeing without hating. In the midst of all the hot words and unmoving positions, they were willing to discuss together. Paul, for example, although he was certain that he was right, refused to act unilaterally. The Antioch congregation refused to separate itself from the Jerusalem congregation. Paul's party refused to disavow the circumcision party. Even after the council gave Paul's group a clear-cut victory, it refused to pass a motion censuring the circumcision party leaders.

Undoubtedly, such an intense controversy left deep hurts. Probably many church members felt alienated from others. Although self-interest and factionalism had wounded the church, the Jerusalem Council allowed the Spirit to renew the fellowship, and steps were taken to heal any divisions before Paul left Jerusalem.

First the assembly deputized Judas Barsabbas and Silas as its agents in Antioch, the Christian center of the north. Next, the assembly sent a letter to be read in Gentile congregations.

The strong similarities between this letter and the Epistle of James indicate that James had a hand in composing the Jerusalem Council letter to the Gentile congregations. Both letters start with a brief introduction, identifying the sender; both letters—the only two to do so in the New Testament—open with the word, "Greeting" (JAMES 1:1, ACTS 15:23). Both letters are irenic in tone; both address the readers as "brethren."

The theme of the Jerusalem letter can be summed up in the opening line: "The brethren . . . to the brethren." (ACTS 15:23) What more beautiful or meaningful way of saying what had to be said! The letter refers to "our beloved Barnabas and Paul" (ACTS 15:25) and recognizes that they had literally risked their lives for the sake of the gospel.

Armed with this conciliatory note, the foursome arrived at Antioch. As official emissaries from the council, Silas and Judas Barsabbas speak authoritatively of the decision reached. Paul and Barnabas, of course, were already committed to the agreement reached.

When there is harmony within the church, the Spirit makes men want to clap their hands with gladness. Appropriately, Luke says that Antioch Christians, hearing the news of peace from Jerusalem, "rejoiced!" (ACTS 15:31)

17

"COME OVER TO MACEDONIA"

(ACTS 15:36 - 16:12)

AFTER THE CIRCUMCISION CONTROVERSY, THE MOOD OF THE CHURCH was to pause and catch its breath. For everyone, that is, except Paul. Restless to push forward, anxious to nurture the frail congregations he left behind in hostile Derbe, Lystra, Iconium, and Pisidian Antioch, Paul proposed, "Come, let us return and visit the brethren in every city where we proclaimed the word of the Lord, and see how they are." (ACTS 15:36)

Plans for the follow-up tour were short-circuited, however, when the subject of John Mark came up. Paul, who had been irked that Mark had left halfway through the first trip, made up his mind that he would not take any chances with him a second time. Barnabas, unperturbed by Mark's defection, firmly insisted that the young man be given another chance. When Paul indignantly refused, the two long-time friends quarrelled.

After sticking together through so much, it seems shameful for Paul and Barnabas to split over such a minor matter. Being human, both were to blame. Our hearts side with Barnabas; our heads, with Paul.

Probably there was more to the disagreement than merely the question of taking Mark. We know from Galatians 2 that Paul was disappointed when Barnabas allowed himself to be swayed by the circumcision party at Antioch before the Council of Jerusalem. Barnabas, perhaps not wanting to offend the traditionalists, had separated himself from eating with Gentile believers at that time. Shocked and hurt at Barnabas' vacillation, Paul undoubtedly felt a certain coolness toward his former companion.

In spite of the falling out, there was no permanent animosity between Paul and Barnabas. Paul obviously quickly forgot the squabble, possibly thinking that he might have been hot-headed and hasty. In subsequent writings, he wrote affectionately of Barnabas. And further, from the references to Mark in Paul's letters (COLOSSIANS 4:10-11; PHILEMON 24; II TIMOTHY 4:11), we know that Paul and Mark became warmly reconciled.

Barnabas returned to Cyprus, where he makes his exit from Acts. Tradition says that he served his remaining years on his native island as a beloved Christian leader. In spite of the dissension between Barnabas and Paul, the church should never forget its debt to Barnabas as the man who twice saved Paul for the church—once at Jerusalem and once at Tarsus.

Looking for a new colleague, Paul turned to Silas, an ideal choice. A man raised in Hebrew traditions, Silas held a prominent position in the Jerusalem church and served as one of the two delegates sent by his home congregation to Antioch after the Jerusalem Council. With such credentials, Silas could quiet any suspicions and heal any hostility.

Apprehensive about the clusters of Christians hanging on precariously in the north, Paul and Silas hurried to Syria and Cilicia. Because Cilicia was Paul's home country, he undoubtedly felt a personal responsibility to work there "strengthening the churches." (ACTS 15:41)

Constantly on the move, the missionary pair climbed the narrow split between the huge shoulders of the Taurus mountains known as the Cilician Gates and entered the desolate plateau where Paul and Barnabas had met with such rebuffs on Paul's first journey. This time, however, Paul reversed the order of the cities he visited because he was nearer to Derbe and Lystra after traveling through the Cilician Gates.

Being human, Paul must have felt some trepidation as he reentered Lystra. Perhaps he still felt aches from the stoning on his first visit. Lystra, however, gave Paul not only one of his closest collisions with death but one of his closest companions in life. A young Lystran Christian, Timothy, son of a prominent Greek pagan father and a devout Jewish mother, became as near to Paul as one of his own family.

Paul and Silas needed a helper. There had been no replacement for Mark. They asked Timothy to accompany them, and he agreed.

It must have been a wrench for both Timothy's mother, Eunice, and Timothy himself to prepare to embark on such a desperately dangerous career. No doubt, Eunice and Timothy had a vivid recollection of Paul's unconscious, blood-caked body crumpled on the city dump and knew that the same fate could easily befall any Christian missionary.

Before Paul, Silas, and Timothy left Lystra, Paul did a surprising thing. He had Timothy, son of a mixed marriage, circumcised. Why, after the mighty ruckus over circumcision ending in the decree of the Council of Antioch, did Paul feel this to be necessary? Was this not a compromise of convictions on his part?

The reasons were strictly practical, not theological. Paul, Silas, and Timothy knew that Timothy's usefulness among hostile synagogue-goers would be impaired unless he was marked with the sign of the covenant. An uncircumcised person was such an offense in some quarters that all doors to communication slammed shut immediately. Paul realized that he would have to adopt certain harmless customs, in this case circumcision, to give him a better entree. Missionaries today do the same; for example, knowing how offensive pigs are to Moslems, no sensitive missionary in Moslem areas flaunts his Christian freedom by eating pork.

Paul was not making circumcision a prerequisite to salvation any more than abstaining from pork would be for us today. Nor was he placating the circumcision party. Circumstances simply made it advisable to have Timothy circumcised in order to help further the spread of the gospel.

Why Timothy, and not Titus?

Paul had already won his point. The Jerusalem Council had resolved that circumcision was not necessary for salvation. Once the church agreed on this, Paul was free to get back to the vital work of evangelism. Circumcision was no longer a doctrinal matter at all in the church, whereas in the case of Titus, it had been. Prior to the council, Paul had refused to circumcise Titus. In Timothy's case, *after* the Jerusalem Council, circumcision made no difference whatsoever to Timothy's standing before God or in the church. It was simply a practical consideration in carrying out the job of ministry.

Paul's party toured the cities where Paul had founded congregations on his first tour, building up and telling these churches of the decision of the council. After leaving the area of Lystra, Iconium, and Pisidian Antioch (the region of Phrygia and Galatia, ACTS 16:6) the trio's plans changed drastically several times. From "the region of Phrygia and Galatia," the map shows the route zigzagging violently over Asia Minor to the city of Troas. The party headed northeastward for about a hundred miles, stopped abruptly, took a long jog southeastward, suddenly shifted direction again, headed due north, unexplainably altered course still another time and took a final leg west. Why did Paul's plans change so radically, causing them to head off on what seem on the map to be such wild goose chases?

Why did God close all the doors to Paul, Silas, and Timothy in Asia Minor? They must have been bewildered at having their prayers answered by such a resounding NO. Turned down everywhere, they sat at Troas, wondering about the Holy Spirit's seemingly capricious ways.

We never quite understand that God sometimes says, "No!" Some of His greatest saints have heard His "No," have wept and wondered, cursed and complained, only to give humble thanks later for the better plans God had in mind all the time. David Livingstone had his heart set on going to China, and was bitterly disappointed until it became clear that he was being led instead to Africa. Sheldon Jackson, diminutive and frail, was turned down by the Presbyterian Board of Foreign Missions, but later gave thanks for this "No" when he was sent to open up mission work in the American northwest and Alaska, gaining the title "Apostle to all beyond."

"And a vision appeared to Paul in the night . . ." Luke relates. A man from Macedonia spoke to Paul in his dream beseeching, "Come over to Macedonia and help us." (ACTS 16:9)

Suddenly in the next sentence the account takes on dramatic new meaning. "And when he had seen the vision," Luke states, "Immediately we sought to go on into Macedonia, concluding that God had called us to preach the gospel to them." (ACTS 16:10) Note that Luke says "we" and "us"—with the abrupt shift from "they" to "we," the picture focuses sharply. The narrative is in the first person, an eye-witness account. Luke is now part of the party.

How did Luke come to join Paul, Silas, and Timothy? Had he previously known Paul? Was he perhaps once a fellow student at Tarsus? Had Paul previously needed medical help and met Luke somewhere in his travels? Did they first meet at Troas? Was Luke the "man from Macedonia"?

Tantalizing though these questions are, we are kept guessing. Many scholars, however, hypothesize that Luke was, in fact, the Macedonian who pleaded so insistently to the reluctant Paul that his appeal even turned up in Paul's dreams.

Paul himself received the answer to his question, "Why did the Holy Spirit not allow me 'to speak the word in Asia' or 'to go into Bithynia'?" The Spirit had bigger plans in mind all the time. Paul, Silas, Timothy, and Luke could only conclude "that God had called us to preach the gospel to them" in Macedonia.

The description of the party's trip from Troas to Macedonia is low-keyed. They were conscious only of traveling from one province to another. Apparently, they had no awareness of the drama of taking the gospel from the East across to the West, from Asia to Europe. Eager to get busy again after the forced inactivity at Troas and the fruitless wandering over northern Asia Minor, they thought mostly of organizing new congregations. Although traveling through some of the most fabulously beautiful scenery in the world, they penned not one word about the Aegean Island crossing. On no pleasure cruise, Paul and his companions were intent on hurrying to work.

On that momentous day, the church jumped the Bosphorus. The Spirit carried the Good News of Jesus Christ across another boundary. No longer would the gospel be regarded as a Middle Eastern cult. God's message through Jesus Christ henceforth would be world-embracing!

18

SINGING IN JAIL AT MIDNIGHT

(ACTS 16: 12-40)

PAUL, SILAS, AND TIMOTHY DID NOT LINGER AT THE PORT OF NEAPO-lis, congratulating themselves on being the first to carry the gospel to Europe or reflecting on what later generations would say about their epochal crossing. They immediately stepped out on the great Roman East-West Road, the famous Egnatian Way uniting Asia with Europe, and headed for the first city, Philippi.

Philippi, a one-time military post colonized by Roman veterans, put on all the airs of Rome itself. Just as colonial cities in the British Empire such as Salisbury, Victoria, Hong Kong, and Singapore proudly copied the architecture, traditions, and even the cricket clubs of London, so Philippi self-consciously made itself into a little Rome, even naming its magistrates "praetores."

Although brought to the area by "a man from Macedonia," Paul's first convert was a woman. And this first convert in Europe was a woman from Asia, from Thyatira, in the very area where Paul had been forbidden to enter!

Proud and powerful though Philippi was, it had no Jewish synagogue. To find some Jews among which to work, Paul and his party had to wait until the Sabbath and hunt the handful of faithful gathered for prayer. As expected, the group was near a stream, in keeping with Levitical purification ceremonies. Not as expected, the praying group was made up of women. The leading spirit in this women's prayer meeting on the river bank outside Philippi was a well-to-do business woman named Lydia, who hailed from the province of the same name. Her home town was Thytira, famous for its expensive purple cloth. Purple, which was highly prized by the ancients, was obtained from an involved process of squeezing the dye from tiny marine life. Lydia, probably in the import business, was comfortably fixed.

Although not born a Jew, she had undoubtedly heard the Old

Testament promise in her home town and had become affiliated with the synagogue. Each Sabbath, even at Philippi, she brought her household for prayers in the ancient tradition.

Lydia, her household, and the other women listened intently to Paul, Silas, Timothy, and Luke. This first European congregation foreshadowed the new role that women would come to play in the world because of Jesus Christ and symbolized the vital part which women would have in the church in the West.

Lydia and her household asked to be baptized. Was her household her children, her staff, or her servants? Were Euidoia and Syntyche, two women who were squabbling when Paul later wrote his letter to the church at Philippi, members of Lydia's household?

The point is that Christianity is a family affair, not exclusively individualistic. Paul constantly refers to families of believers, such as "the household of Stephanas" (I CORINTHIANS 1:16; 16:15), "Chloe's people (I CORINTHIANS 1:11), Prisca and Aquila and "the church in their house." (ROMANS 16:5) The gospel means that a person is in a new relationship with everyone around him, starting with those under the same roof.

Hospitable and generous, Lydia insisted that Paul's party make her large house its headquarters. Eventually, the congregation that came together regularly at Lydia's was one of the most colorful and varied of any in the history of the church.

The next unexpected addition to the congregation was one of the most unusual, a conversion that literally caused a riot which landed Paul and Silas in jail.

We do not even know her name. She was a slave girl who fell into trances, during which Luke tells us that she "had a spirit of divination." (ACTS 16:16) Luke uses the Greek word "pythonos," referring to the great python or Pythian serpent which once guarded the oracle at Delphi until, in myth, slain by Apollo. To Luke, this was the medical term for weird behavior. To the gullible public, the girl's trances were tied in with the occult.

Actually, of course, there was nothing occult whatsoever. The unfortunate girl was an emotionally disturbed personality, perhaps a schizophrenic. In any case, her malady was cruelly exploited by her owners. Led around as an animal, treated as a freak, the girl's serious condition was aggravated to the point of being chronic.

Apparently in a long trance, she continually followed Paul, Silas, Timothy, and Luke. Nearly every time they tried to speak, she interrupted, shrieking loudly, "These men are servants of the Most High God, who proclaim to you the way of salvation." (ACTS 16:17)

It was impossible to compete with such a nuisance and Paul finally had enough. His ire, however, was directed not at the girl herself but at "the spirit" (ACTS 16:18) possessing her. Charging it to let go and leave, Paul brought her release and healing.

Until recently, we must remember, even the most sophisticated believed in demon possession. In fact, we still say such things as, "He seems like one possessed," and "I don't know what got into him," and "He is not himself today." Medical knowledge, especially in treating emotional disorders in the first century, believed that healing took place when unclean spirits were removed.

No longer a slave to schizophrenia or whatever her ailment was, the slave girl was now a servant to Jesus Christ. To her owners, however, she was useless.

Taking matters into their own hands, the owners of the slave girl grabbed Paul and Silas and manhandled them before the civil magistrates. In the uproar, the inevitable crowd collected. Playing on the prejudices of the mob, the owners shouted, "These men are Jews and they are disturbing our city. They advocate customs which it is not lawful for us Romans to accept or practice." (ACTS 16:20-21)

In Philippi, so self-consciously Roman, the super-patriots held the Emperor-cult in highest honor. Paul's activities were quickly construed to be an affront to the Emperor himself.

The crowd, ever-ready in any age to boil up when something is presented as unpatriotic, joined the owners in the attack on Paul and Silas. The magistrates, swayed by an obvious dislike of Jews, sympathetic to the slavegirl's owners (undoubtedly the magistrates had been entertained by the girl's performances during her trances) ordered Paul and Silas stripped. Refusing to hear the case further, ignoring Paul and Silas' protests, they nodded to the lictors, policemen with rods for beating.

Paul endured the grisly and degrading ordeal of being beaten by rods twice in his life. Philippi was one time. Being flailed by a big bundle of heavy sticks tied together always left a man's back a horrible pulp and sometimes caused internal hemorrhaging, injuries to organs, smashed vertebrae and broken ribs, and even death. Paul and Silas would not have been pretty sights by the time the lictors finished with them.

Aching, limping, and bleeding, Paul and Silas were dragged to the Philippi prison; they were pushed into the dark, stifling cell farthest from light or air, their legs securely locked into stocks to prevent escape or movement. Lice, rats, and disease infested first century prisons; prisoners were forced to exist in their own filth. Paul and Silas quickly found their legs growing stiff from being pinned in one position by the stocks. They grew weak from hunger. Their bodies throbbed with pain from the beating. Sleep was impossible.

Paul and Silas probably comforted themselves that they were part of the glorious company of God's witnesses who have been thrown into places of confinement. They did not cower in defeat or snivel with self-pity, shriek curses at the jailor nor protest the outrage. Instead, they prayed and sang hymns.

The first thing that strikes us about these two prisoners' behavior is their cheerfulness. They exuded joy even in jail, maintaining optimism when there seemed to be no hope left.

What did Paul and Silas sing? Their hymns are usually believed to be selections from PSALMS 113-118, great paens of praise to God, who can be trusted to act.

Men who sing cannot be stopped. Kermit Eby, a student of the American labor movement, observes that in the early days of the unions in this country, the workers sang. Eby notes that later, after gains were made, the singing gradually died. Today, at union meetings, songs are seldom sung by the rank and file.

Christianity has always been a singing faith. The great hymns of our forebears attest to this: the solemnity and virility of the psalm tunes on the Galloway moors or French countryside; the grace and power of the Wesleyan hymns soaring from English slums; the dignity and authority of the German chorales lifting from Rhineland chapels; the intensity and vigor of Welsh canticles rising from mountain coal slashes.

Paradoxically, we who have more to sing about than anyone else grow faint-hearted at expressing our faith in music; the Holy Spirit means for us to *sing,* not timidly mouth words.

Luke tells us that as Paul and Silas sang, ". . . the prisoners were listening. . . ." (ACTS 16:25) Aware that others were straining for some word of hope, Paul and Silas continued to witness to Jesus Christ—even in jail!

Taking the cue from Paul and Silas, we know that we are called to serve in whatever circumstances we find ourselves—even within the grey walls of everyday life.

As the imprisoned pair sang, suddenly the entire building began to shudder. The deep rumble of an earthquake silenced the psalm.

Screams of terror, the crash of falling beams, the roar of collapsing masonry followed. As the dust settled, Paul and Silas discovered that the bolts holding the stocks to the wall had been loosened and the cell door had been shaken open. They could have fled in the confusion. Instead of a secret escape, however, they stayed to look after their panic-stricken fellow prisoners.

Roused by the earthquake, the jailer rushed into the ruined cell block in a state of shock. Possibly he had heard of the slave girl's testimony about Paul and Silas and thought that the earthquake was a divine omen. Certain that his prisoners had escaped, the jailer lost his head. Apparently holding the Roman notion that death was better than disgrace, with desperate resignation the jailer drew his dagger to stab himself. Philippi, noted in ancient times for its high suicide rate, was the place where Cassius and Brutus had set a sort of morbid example in saving face by taking their own lives. The jailer was ready to follow suit.

Paul and Silas were the only calm voices in the uproar and panic. With a blend of common sense and compassion, Paul yelled that everyone was present and that the jailer should put away his dagger.

Shaking with terror, the jailer knelt before Paul and Silas and gasped, "Men, what must I do to be saved?" (ACTS 16:30).

Paul had an immediate answer: "Believe in the Lord Jesus and you will be saved." Noting that the jailer's family had crowded around, Paul added, "You and your household." (ACTS 16:31)

This is the only response to the jailer's question. Even when the question may be worded in more sophisticated language, we, like Paul, can unequivocably point to Jesus Christ and plead for trust in Him personally.

The jailer was given back his life that night. More perhaps than anyone in Philippi he knew personally that Jesus Christ had saved him.

Gratefully, he cleaned up Paul's and Silas' wounds, took them to his quarter, and had a meal prepared for them. Undoubtedly, a long, searching conversation took place during the early hours over the table, concluding when the jailer asked to be baptized with his family. There were two washings that night. The first was when the jailer made his captives' wounds clean, the second when the captives made the jailer's life clean.

At daylight, police knocked at the door, reporting that the magistrates had reversed themselves and wanted Paul and Silas to leave town as quickly and quietly as possible. Probably upset by the earthquake and superstitiously inclined to attribute this disaster to the displeasure of some deity connected with Paul's group, the officials wanted to hustle the strangers out of jail and on their way before some new catastrophe hit.

Both Paul and Silas were Roman citizens. Standing their ground, they made clear that their personal rights had been seriously violated the previous day. Stunned, the police reported this to the magistrates, who immediately hurried in person to make official apologies. Both magistrates and prisoners knew well that the procedures the day before were flagrantly illegal. Two bedrock rights of Roman citizens had been violated: No citizen could be punished without a trial, and no citizen could be beaten with rods.

Paul and Silas were not making such an issue out of the case because of an outraged sense of honor or injured dignity. Rather, they wanted to protect the new believers in Philippi from possible future danger from mobs or injustice from the magistrates. A public beating was such a disgrace that it would stigmatize the young congregation. Paul and Silas were determined to set the record straight so that the public would not be prejudiced against Christians. Paul's motives were to help the church gain acceptance in Philippi.

At the same time, Paul and Silas did not press charges against the red-faced magistrates as they could have done. Conviction would have thrown these magistrates out of office and prevented them from ever again holding any governmental office. Not anxious to leave behind a residue of resentment toward the gospel, Paul and Silas let the matter drop after the magistrates apologized, undoubtedly, gaining the respect and sympathy of both the magistrates and the general public.

Paul and Silas revisited Lydia and the others in the new Philippi Christian congregation. Paul subsequently felt a special affection for this loyal group. As unlikely and as unhomogenous a gathering as it was—a wealthy business woman, an ex-slave girl known for strange trances, the keeper of the city jail, a physician, and others—this congregation became renowned for its hospitality and generosity. Paul wrote later how the Philippian church repeatedly sent him money and spoke of the members as people "whom I love and long for, my joy and my crown. . . ." (PHILLIPPIANS 4:1)

Leaving behind Timothy and Luke to build up this fascinating and promising congregation, Paul and Silas took to the Great East-West Road again.

19

THE NOT-SO-REASONABLE GOSPEL

(ACTS 17)

THE STORY OF THE TRIP THROUGH MACEDONIA WAS BEGINNING TO sound like the first missionary journey when Paul and Barnabas hit the cities of southern Asia Minor. The pattern was much the same: brief, vigorous work beginning with the synagogues as a seedbed, the inevitable intense opposition followed by the hurried departure.

\There was, however, one difference. On this trip, Paul's strategy was to work only in the large cities. Far ahead of his time in realizing that the metropolitan centers create tastes and spawn new ideas, Paul skipped Amphipolis and Apollonia after leaving Philippi. Spaced at approximate thirty mile intervals, Amphipolis and Apollonia made convenient overnight stopovers for Paul, Timothy, and Silas. The party, aiming at the Macedonian capital, hurried on.

According to Strabo, the first century historian, Thessalonica, capital of the province, was the largest city in Macedonia and the business and commercial center of Greece. It also had the distinction of the status of a "free city" under Rome, meaning that no Roman soldiers were garrisoned there, it was completely self-governing, did not have to display any Roman insignia in the street and had other unusual rights.

Paul, Silas, and Timothy, refusing to take advantage of the generosity of Luke or Lydia or others at Philippi, insisted on earning their own way. Living with working people as working men themselves, the evangelists rose daily before dawn to put in a hard day's labor before starting their teaching and preaching. A few months later, writing from Corinth to the Thessalonian Christians, Paul reminded them that he had worked with his hands and advised them not to be parasites but to be willing to work if they wanted to eat. (I THESSALONIANS 4:11; II THESSALONIANS 3:8-10)

Realizing that the Jewish community provided the likeliest starting point for a cell of new Christians, the trio spent most of their energies

133

on the synagogue. Each afternoon and evening, working with Scriptures, they discussed the meaning of God's work in Jesus Christ. It is worthwhile to note that these sessions were never high-pressure, hysteria-charged revival meetings. Instead of relying on emotionalism, the visitors and the synagogue attenders carefully sifted the Scriptures, allowing the Holy Spirit to have His say as the group addressed itself to the Bible. Evangelism at its best, this technique allowed the Spirit to make Jesus Christ real and relevant to everyone —almost.

There was a small core of a die-hard reactionaries. Bitter that Gentiles were not second-class believers, according to the New Promise, but were welcomed on an equal footing, these super-Jews forgot their father's faith and resorted to an underhanded attack.

On any waterfront even today, it is easy to collect the rabble for mob action from the wharf cafes, docks, and street corners. Thessalonica had its share of loafers, misfits, and disgruntled who could be manipulated by any loud-mouthed agitator.

Branding the visiting Christians as dangerous subversives, clever rabble-rousers quickly whipped up a mob. The blow-torch oratory sent the crowds raging through the streets to the house of Jason, where Paul's party was staying. Providentially, Paul and Silas and Timothy were out, else the outcome of Acts might have been much different.

Out for blood and angry at not finding its quarry, the mob ransacked the house and seized Jason and a few others. Perhaps Jason had got wind of what was up and had hidden Paul, Silas, and Timothy. Undoubtedly saving these three from a severe mauling or possibly lynching, Jason took the brunt of the mob's fury.

Dragged before the magistrates, Jason allowed his reputation to be smeared to protect the visiting Christians. He had to listen to reckless charges which were ticklish to refute, and to endure the humiliation which a public hearing always brought. Posting bond, he made an additional sacrifice of money (he had already seen his house and possessions wrecked). As a resident of Thessalonica, he knew that he would have to stay on after Paul's group left, live down the disgrace, ignore the gossip, offset the bad name, recoup his losses.

The charges against Jason and the other Christians were serious. "These men who have turned the world upside down have come here also," the accusation ran, "and Jason has received them; and they are all acting against the decrees of Caesar, saying that there is another king, Jesus." (ACTS 17:6-9)

134

Thessalonica, as a "Free City," was frantically anxious to keep its proud title. The magistrates were touchy about anyone's casting slurs on the Emperor for fear Rome would consider taking back all its privileges.

It was easy to see how casual listeners could pick up these ideas about Christians. In the Bible study in the synagogue, Paul and Silas spoke of God's promise having come to pass when Jesus Christ came. Words in the Christian vocabulary such as "Kingly power," "Ruler," "Kingdom" could easily have had a seditious sound to a suspicious mind. Putting Jesus ahead of the Emperor, hostile people reasoned, was traitors' talk.

"Men who have turned the world upside down!" What an impact these Spirit-filled, Spirit-led men made! Fired by the Spirit, they presented the news of God's action in Jesus Christ in such a way that the world really *would* flip if it took Him seriously. The gospel was radical. Its challenge chopped at the roots of everything Thessalonica took seriously!

"There is another king, Jesus," shrieked the crowd. How right they were! The rival to all the thrones set up by the culture in Thessalonica or in Thompsonville, He claims ultimate and final allegiance. No matter how worthwhile our allegiance to any*thing* or any*one* else, this can only be a number-two loyalty—our first obedience is to "another king, Jesus." Submit to any other, and we find ourselves not serving the king but groveling before a tyrant. Only Jesus Christ can claim our total devotion, yet grant us perfect freedom.

Any time we recognize the claims of this other King, Jesus, look out, Society! The world will be turned upside down again!

After the wild scenes at Jason's house and the hearing chambers, the position of the visiting Christians at Thessalonica was precarious. With synagogue fanatics, mistrustful public officials and hot-tempered mob elements all watching for Paul, Timothy, and Silas, it was best for them to leave town and lie low for a time. Paul particularly was reluctant to leave, because he had enjoyed his work and was looking forward to a fruitful stay at Thessalonica. Disappointed at having to pack up while there was still so much to be done, the group retreated to Beroea, sixty miles away.

Somewhat off the beaten track, perched on the slopes of the Olympian range, Beroea was a quiet minor town supposedly located far enough from Thessalonica to be safe and yet near enough to return as soon as the coast was clear. Paul and Silas apparently were only biding their time when they first went to Beroea. Meanwhile, they used the time to advantage by introducing the local synagogue to the gospel. Just as this group was conscientiously studying their claims about God's mighty deliverance in Jesus Christ, word leaked back to Thessalonica of the pair's activities. It was Phillippi and Thessalonica all over again. Paul as ringleader had to flee; Silas and Timothy were able to remain.

Obviously, it was impossible for Paul to return to Thessalonica. Two routes remained open: over the mountains or down to the coast to catch a ship to the south. Taking the latter course, Paul suddenly found himself on a small vessel bound for Athens.

Athens was a low point, emotionally, in Paul's life. Harried from one city to another, disappointed at the lack of time and opportunities to nourish the infant congregations left behind in the north, apprehensive about the safety of the leaders in those churches, worried about his closest friends, alone and friendless, Paul planned only to wait at Athens for Silas and Timothy to join him.

Sailing into Pireaus, port of Athens, Paul would have seen the gleaming shield, helmet, and spear of the enormous statue of Minerva or Athena on the Acropolis. Walking up the Hamaxitos Road, he would have passed the altars raised at intervals to unknown gods. Wandering through the great city, he would have noticed the lovely porticoes, the shady avenues, the graceful statues, all reflecting the healthy sensualism of the Greeks. Paul must also have gazed up at the Acropolis, that breath-taking blend of architectural design, natural spectacle, and artistic craftsmanship floating above Athens as a vision of gleaming splendor in marble and gold. If the skill of Praxiteles or other gifted geniuses affected Paul, he never mentioned it to anyone.

Athens liked to pride itself on its learning and its religion. The intellectual mecca of the ancient world, the city carried proud memories of Socrates, Plato, Aristotle, and dozens of renowned thinkers. The University called itself "the eye of Greece," "the mother of arts." The clever, witty Athenians, whose forebears had contributed much to human knowledge, enjoyed toying with ideas. Gifted conversationalists, they were genial and tolerant. Posing as "thinkers," they could be categorized for the most part as either "Stoics" or "Epicureans." Basically, the key words of these popular thought systems were *pleasure* for Epicureanism and *pride* for Stoicism. Athens in Paul's day continued to retain its renown for philosophy.

Possibly the most outwardly religious city in the world at the time, Athens offered a home to almost every god in the vast Olympian pantheon. Nearly every public building was actually a shrine—the

Record House, for example, was a temple to the mother of gods, the Council House housed statues to Apollo and Jupiter, the theater at the foot of the Acropolis was consecrated to Bacchus. The magnificent Acropolis itself, the focal point of Athens, was actually a vast and ornate collection of sanctuaries. Everywhere in the city there were shrines and temples, each with magnificently carved statuary, each an architectural masterpiece. There were altars dedicated even to abstractions such as Fame, Energy, Modesty, and Persuasion. Some altars had been erected years before when, during a plague, Epimenides had brought in a flock of black and white sheep, and had ordered a sacrifice and altar on the place wherever a sheep lay down. Athens maintained an aura of reverence for all the Greek myths.

Life, for Athenians, was given over to art and amusements, philosophy and philandering. In spite of the religion and learning saturating the city, Paul was incensed. After whiffing the spiritual atmosphere, Paul was provoked into doing what he had no intention of doing when he arrived: ". . . he preached Jesus and the resurrection." (ACTS 17:18)

Some still wonder why. Does anyone with a knowledge of philosophy need the gospel?

The church has never quite made up its mind on how to regard philosophy. Some within the church, such as the second-century Latin father Tertellian, have snorted that philosophy is "ever handling questions but never settling anything . . . What is there in common between Athens and Jerusalem?" Others such as Clement of Alexandria, living at the same time, have maintained that philosophy "was necessary to the Greeks for righteousness until the coming of the Lord . . . for philosophy was a 'schoolmaster' to bring the Greek mind to Christ . . . a preparation, paving the way toward perfection in Christ." Whether philosophy is a nuisance or a preparation, the church has not been certain. It has, however, rejected the claim that philosophy can be a substitute for the gospel. Every Christian must agree with Paul that thinking great thoughts can never extricate a man from himself.

At Athens on Paul's visit, the cross encountered the academy. God's mighty act, to the sophisticated, supercilious Greeks, was nothing but a lot of foolishness and weakness. Paul's answer, however, should give pause to the philosophers of every age. Referring to the gospel, Paul wrote, ". . . the foolishness of God is wiser than men, and the weakness of God is stronger than men." (I CORINTHIANS 1:25)

At Athens, the cross confronted the cults. In spite of the religious varnish in every cornice of Athenian life, these religions were powerless. The Greek divinities were either processes of nature or deified humans. No matter how idolized, they were unable to save.

The hopeless cycle remained. Assuming for a moment that a man knows what is "good" (a very dangerous assumption), how does he *will* to do what he knows he *should* do? A lifetime of worship at Athens' plethora of altars could not help.

Regardless of all the scholars and shrines, Athens did not want to commit itself to anyone or anything. Philosophy and religion were pastimes, good for an evening's conversation. Paul created a momentary stir by his presentation. The languid intellectuals of the Athens streets were curious. Their attitude toward the gospel, however, was that Paul had an interesting "new teaching" (ACTS 17:19) featuring "foreign divinities." (ACTS 17:18)

Luke uses a bit of Athens street slang to convey what the Athenians thought of Paul himself. A "babbler" was the Athenians' word for Paul. In Greek, it means literally a bird picking first at one seed, then another, and came to be applied to someone hanging about the market, picking up scraps which fell off loads. In intellectual circles, it meant someone who was an idea-scrounger, a person who collected odds and ends of second-hand ideas gleaned from others and peddled these as "knowledge." In other words, the Athenian listeners looked upon Paul as just one more crank philosopher who had wandered into town with some theory or scraps of learning to amuse them.

Athens had an official Board of Inquiry, the Areopagus—named after the rocky prominence—which checked out teachers and speakers in the city. Paul's appearance before the Areopagus was not a trial, but simply a presentation of a summary of his teaching for that body to hear.

Some of Paul's critics have ripped Paul for his speech before the Areopagus, claiming that it contained little that was distinctively Christian and sounded more like a lecture on the philosophy of religion.

Did he water down the content of the gospel to make a more appealing appearance? A careful reading of Paul's address (ACTS 17:22-31) shows that Paul held to the essentials of the faith. However, the speech also reflects a self-conscious attempt to be sophisticated. Although from a technical standpoint the address is a masterpiece, showing that Paul was a cultured, gifted man of learning, from a homiletic standpoint, it was a dud.

In the tradition of Demosthenes and the Greek orators, Paul

138

opened with "Men of Athens" and complimented his hearers with the usual delicate flourishes of a man of good taste. He even embellished his remarks with a graceful quotation from the Stoic poets Aratus, Phaenomena, and Cleanthes' "Hymn to Love" showing that he was no mere "babbler" or "seedpicker" but a refined scholar who could refer to the classics if he wanted.

Gradually Paul worked around to the subject at hand. Reporting that he had seen an altar inscribed "To an unknown god," Paul spoke eloquently on the subject of man's search for God. All people, asserted Paul, "seek God, in the hope that they might feel after him" (ACTS 17:27) and used the Greek word to describe a man groping in the dark which Plato in his "Phaedo" used to refer to a vague guess at truth.

Waving his hand at the opulence everywhere around the audience, Paul exclaimed, "Being then God's offspring, we ought not to think that the Deity is like gold, or silver, or stone, a representation by the art and imagination of man." (ACTS 17:29)

Paul then shifted gears, swiftly moving his hearers from generalities about the Deity to the God who has decisively involved Himself through the resurrection of Jesus Christ, the living God, who will judge the entire universe.

Resurrection from the dead? Suddenly Paul's audience hooted with laughter. Ridiculous! How could anyone be serious, they howled. A few politely said to Paul, "We will hear you again about this." (ACTS 17:32) Whatever Paul had planned to say in the remainder of his address is now lost. His day before the Areopagus ended as a fiasco.

A handful remained and became believers. Among them was one convert of distinction, a member of the Areopagus named Dionysius, later the legendary bishop of Athens, and an otherwise unknown woman named Damaris.

Why was there such poor success at Athens? Perhaps it is significant that Athens, the place where Paul met with such disappointing failure, was also the only place where Paul did not meet with persecution. Instead of persecuting Paul, Athens gave a bored yawn.

Paul, however, blamed himself. Re-examining his work at Athens, he went back over his presentation before the Areopagus. Noting in his own mind that he had dressed up his speech to appeal to the intelligentsia of Athens, Paul told himself that he had tried to make the gospel sound reasonable. Arty, polished, and logical though he had been, Paul felt a deep sense of failure—there simply were no logical arguments for the cross and resurrection.

Wandering on to Corinth, Paul made up his mind firmly to skip the frills in his preaching. Henceforth, he promised himself, he would concentrate starkly and bluntly on the news that can never be made to appear sweet and reasonable.

Paul never visited Athens again. Nor did he ever write an "Epistle to the Athenians." Humbled by the Spirit, he was prepared, however, for even greater service—the ministry at Corinth and the beginning of his letter writing.

20

"WE HAVE NEVER EVEN HEARD THAT THERE IS A HOLY SPIRIT"

(ACTS 18:1-19:7)

WISE SKIPPERS SAILING FROM THE ADRIATIC TO THE AEGEAN SEA could steer clear of the treacherous waters around Cape Malea on the southernmost tip of Greece, thanks to the fact that nature had provided a two hundred mile shortcut. Most mariners took this detour, sailing up the straits on either side of a narrow waist of land. The passage on the west from the Adriatic was called the Gulf of Corinth; that on the east, the Saronic Gulf. This strategic isthmus was blessed with two of the few decent harbors anywhere in southern Greece— Lechaeum on the west side and, a few miles across land, Cenchrae on the east. Ships would sail into either port, unload their cargoes, have them carried across the isthmus and reloaded on the other side. Frequently the ships themselves were dragged across the narrow neck of land on rollers and refloated in the opposite harbor. (Today, there is a ship canal. Proposed by Julius Caesar and begun by Nero, the canal did not become a reality until 1893!)

Nature further blessed this strategic site with one of the world's few great natural fortresses. Towering over the area is a two-thousand foot high, Gibralter-like block, wide enough on top to put an entire city.

With such endowments any city would become rich and powerful, and Corinth was no exception. Called "the city of the two seas" by the poets, Corinth rose to become one of the great maritime powers in the ancient world. From Corinth's drawing boards and shipyards came the first triremes, the dreadnought of the Greek-Roman world, ranking the Corinthians with the Phoenicians as the best nautical designers of the Mediterranean. Corinth was depicted allegorically in carvings as a woman on a rock before two other figures, each holding a rudder, boasting that Corinth was "prow and stern of Greece."

141

Much as Corinth might have liked to call itself the prow and rudder of Greece, to the rest of the world it was the sinkhole of vice of the Roman Empire. Like every busy port, Corinth caught the human scourings. The wild debauchery that took place at Corinth, however, made even the blasé Greeks blush. So notorious were the sexual excesses at Corinth that the phrase, "to live like a Corinthian," became synonomous for loose morals. The wide-open, year-around Fair and the hustling temple prostitutes at the great shrine to Aphrodite on top of the great rock or acropolis laughed at chastity.

⸜Corinth was the last place on earth that anyone would have thought of trying to start a church. Paul, depressed after the fizzle at Athens, tired after the beatings, jailing, threats, and flights in the north, wandered into town while waiting for word to return to Macedonia. No congregation was planned. It probably appeared hopeless.

Finding a Jewish cloth-weaving couple, Aquila and Priscilla, recently expelled from Rome, Paul picked up his old trade to earn a living. There was no salary from Antioch, no help from the other churches, and Paul worked for his keep.

Almost in spite of himself, Paul found himself pushed by the Spirit into part-time preaching at the local synagogue. Later, after Silas and Timothy joined Paul, the appeal at the synagogue was stepped up until opposition forced them to shift to the Gentiles. A handful of Jews, including Crispus, the former president of the synagogue, followed the missionaries as they moved next door to the house of another convert, Titius Justus. Before anyone realized it, a Christian congregation came into being in the city where everybody agreed it could never happen.

The little church flourished. ". . . Many of the Corinthians hearing Paul believed and were baptized." (ACTS 18:8) But fresh from their vices, immersed in an easy-going culture, many of these Corinthian Christians found it hard to shake off their pagan ways. Although Acts is silent on the subject, from the content and volume of the correspondence Paul had with the congregation, it is obvious that ⸜Corinth was Paul's "problem church."

Paul and his companions managed to log eighteen months at Corinth—a record in any city since leaving Antioch. It was not, however, an easy, pleasant year-and-a-half. Several times violence threatened to flare, and, jumpy after so many beatings and jailings, Paul was tempted to slip away.

The Holy Spirit refused to let Paul step out. Strengthening Paul to stay, He said, "Do not be afraid, but speak and do not be silent; for I am with you, and no man shall attack you to harm you; for I have many people in this city." (ACTS 18:9)

As a reminder of the Spirit's promise to deliver him safely from Corinth, Paul vowed to let his hair grow. Later, at the port of Cenchrae before leaving Corinth, he finally cut his hair, recognizing that God kept His word and giving thanks for safe deliverance.

There was at least one close call when it seemed that the Holy Spirit was not going to keep His word. The synagogue crowd dusted off the same charges concocted at Philippi and Thessalonica against Paul, pulling him into court. Fortunately, the proconsul of the province of Achaia who heard the charges was a forthright, upstanding Roman named Gallio, who asked the accusers what specific law they accused Paul of breaking. Learning that they were charging Paul with breaking Jewish law, Gallio refused to get embroiled in the dispute and dismissed the case. Gallio, in fact, so pointedly snubbed the synagogue troublemakers that the rowdy spectators outside the court chambers later roughed up Sosthenes, the synagogue's spokesman.

Gallio was a well-known, deeply respected attorney and government official who served as proconsul of Achaia from A.D. 44 for many years. As the brother of the famous writer and philosopher Seneca, he had good connections. His part in Acts was undoubtedly played up deliberately by Luke. We recall that Luke was writing to Theophilus, who, many scholars believe, was himself a Roman government official. Out of deference to Theophilus, Luke went out of his way to show (1) that the church did not indict every Roman government man, and (2) that at least one well-placed official saw how patently false the charges were that Christians were law breakers and subversives.

Why did Paul leave Corinth? No reasons are given in Acts. The best hypothesis seems to be that Paul wanted to return to Jerusalem for one of the great celebrations. Undoubtedly he felt that the congregation could survive without his presence. There were others such as Stephanas and Erastus, as well as Crispus and Titius Justus, who formed the nucleous of the generous, albeit shaky congregation.

After completing his vow and clipping his hair, Paul sailed from Cenchrae for Jerusalem. Aquila and Priscilla, his cloth-weaving associates at Corinth, went with him as far as Ephesus.

The traffic between Corinth and Ephesus, the two great mercantile ports of the Aegean, was comparable to the crossing between New York and Southampton, and Aquila and Priscilla probably had business to attend to at Ephesus. Paul paid a brief visit to the synagogue,

143

promised to return, and sailed for Caesarea on the coast of Palestine, nearest port to Jerusalem.

Luke gives sketchy details about Paul's itinerary, stating only, "When he had landed at Caesarea, he went up and greeted the church, and then went down to Antioch." (ACTS 18:22) The Greek verb, "he went up" clearly implies that Paul actually traveled to Jerusalem. For Passover? The Feast of Tabernacles? A friendly meeting with James and/or Peter? Luke, however, is not writing a biography of Paul.

Telescoping what must have been an eventful, exciting odyssey by Paul through Antioch, Galatia, and Phrygia (the latter two were districts in Asia Minor) into one sentence, Luke skips back to Ephesus to show what the Holy Spirit was doing there.

Our scene is Ephesus, where Paul had stopped briefly to tell the synagogue of the Messiah's coming, the Promise fulfillment. Aquila and Priscilla, staying on, had quietly kept alive the idea which Paul had planted.

One day, a young man turned up at the Ephesus synagogue. Named Apollos, this young Jew began to speak eloquently and fervently about Jesus. Trained in the excellent schools of rhetoric in his home town, Alexandria, Egypt, Apollos was a forceful orator and skilled debater who made a powerful impression.

Aquila and Prescilla listened. They were disquieted—for all of Apollos' talk about Jesus, there were certain glaring gaps in his understanding of the gospel.

Luke says that Apollos "had been instructed in the way of the Lord . . . though he knew only the baptism of John." (ACTS 18:25) "Instructed" can mean in the Greek "catechized," suggesting that Apollos had had a formal course on the life of Jesus, possibly having heard about Jesus from one of the catechists or teachers sent from Jerusalem to Egypt. He may even have got hold of some brief piece of Christian writing, since the earliest written materials were beginning to circulate about that time.

All this was fine, but it did not go far enough. Apollos had primarily a textbook knowledge of Jesus. He had heard many, many facts about Jesus, took them seriously, agreed that Jesus was indeed the Promised One of Israel, and argued the point persuasively.

Apollos had even been baptized, but his baptism was the old baptism of repentance used by John the Baptist, and actually the ancient Essene self-cleansing ceremony. Apollos had never been touched by the Holy Spirit.

144

As a Christian, a person must be informed about the facts of our faith. It is vital, however, to be more than an informed person. Until a man has his own personal Pentecost, he can at best only partially understand what God has done for man through Jesus Christ's life, death, and resurrection and through the coming of the Spirit to the disciples.

Apollos had read the right books and listened to the best lectures, but in reality this young man "knew" less than two untutored, itinerant cloth weavers! Unbaptized by the Holy Spirit, Apollos' grasp of God's news was inadequate and incomplete.

Aquila and Priscilla, grateful that God had raised up such a promising young leader, at the same time were disturbed. What should they say or do?

As any wise and older saint knows, it is a ticklish job to work with a young seminary graduate. Offended sensibilities can easily produce extended hostilities.

Aquila and Priscilla managed to work with Apollos, correcting and encouraging. Gently and patiently, ". . . they took him and expounded to him the way of God more accurately." (ACTS 18:26)

How frequently God uses an Aquila and Priscilla to counsel a fledgling preacher! What would the church be without godly laymen such as this pair of quiet cloth weavers! Though no speakers themselves, Aquila and Priscilla knew when to speak to a would-be spokesman.

Shortly afterwards, Apollos sailed from Ephesus to Corinth, carrying letters of introduction to the young congregation on the isthmus. Apollos quickly scored a hit at Corinth. His flashy answers to critics, his artful discourses, his smooth manner soon built him a personal following in the congregation. Apollos, everyone quickly noticed, was different from Paul in many ways—age, appearance, temperament, mannerisms. His oratory especially appealed to the Corinthians, and drew unfavorable comparisons to Paul's. Paul, it will be remembered, threw away his philosophic style after Athens, resolving to speak only of God's act of reconciliation in ungarnished terms.

Inexperienced and unwitting, Apollos allowed himself to be lionized by many in the Corinthian church to the point where a pro-Apollos faction developed against a pro-Paul faction. The rivalry between the "we're Apollos' supporters" versus "we're Paul's" nearly ripped apart the Corinthian church and prompted some blunt warnings on label-wearing in the church by Paul in a letter to the Corinthians.

Through all of the tension caused by the competition between the Apollos party and the Paul faction at Corinth, however, there was no personal animosity whatsoever between Paul and Apollos. Paul referred to Apollos as "our brother." (I CORINTHIANS 16:12)

Not long after Apollos, accompanied by Aquila and Priscilla, left Ephesus and sailed to Corinth, Paul arrived at Ephesus. He was accompanied by Timothy, Erastus, Caius, Aristarchus, and Titus. Paul, who had made a quick stopover at Ephesus on his trip from Corinth to Jerusalem, had planned for some time to launch a full-scale campaign there. The key city of western Asia Minor, Ephesus would be the base from which workers would fan out through the entire area. Paul knew it would not be easy—Ephesus was the catch-basin or all the sects swirling through the Eastern world. He and his party dug in for a long stay. Timothy was sent to nearby Colossae, and others in Paul's party were undoubtedly assigned other cities so that each of the seven great cities of western Asia was covered. The famous "Seven Churches"—Ephesus, Smyrna, Perganum, Thyatira, Sardis, Philadelphia, and Laodicea—came about as a result.

Shortly after his arrival at Ephesus, Paul encountered twelve people who were the imperfect results of Apollos' incomplete preaching. Like Apollos before his instruction by Aquila and Priscilla, they had never received the Holy Spirit, telling Paul, ". . . We have never even heard that there is a Holy Spirit." (ACTS 19:2) Their baptism, like Apollos' originally, had only been the repentance rite of John the Baptist.

Why such an emphasis on the Holy Spirit? Why did Paul insist that these twelve receive the Spirit? Isn't it enough to know something about Jesus and to want to "follow" Him (whatever that means)?

Sometimes we think of the Holy Spirit as an "extra" in the Christian life, much as an accessory which as we may opt to add to a new car.

Apart from the Holy Spirit, these twelve were merely enthusiasts for Jesus. Informed about and interested in the Carpenter from Nazareth, they could speak feelingly of Jesus, the great teacher, the noble rabbi, the best man who had ever lived. This, however, was hero-worship, this was adulation. It was not really an appreciation of what God has done through Jesus' life, death, and resurrection.

God wants us to be more than patrons or enthusiasts. He does not want our applause or endorsement—He has far more in mind. He means to touch us with the Life lived in the crucified, risen Galilean. He wants to transform us from being more than mere boosters; He wants to re-create us into new personalities. There is a vital difference between being a respectful supporter and a reborn sinner, and Paul knew it.

Paul took the twelve half-converted products of Apollos' preaching and patiently unfolded the full dimension of God's acts culminating in the cross, the resurrection, and Pentecost. Ultimately, the dozen asked to be baptized "in the name of the Lord Jesus."

A Pentecost took place at Ephesus for those twelve, "And when Paul had laid his hands upon them, the Holy Spirit came on them. . . ." (ACTS 19:6)

A new outpouring of the Holy Spirit will come any place where we ask for Him.

21

RIOT AND FINAL FAREWELL

(ACTS 19:8 - 20:38)

CENTURIES OLD, SUMPTUOUSLY LAVISH, THE TEMPLE OF DIANA AT
Ephesus was one of the Seven Wonders of the World. The great
temple housed the Treasury, preserved the heritage, and regulated the
customs of Ephesus, not unlike having the Bank of England, West-
minster Abbey, Windsor Castle, and Buckingham Palace all combined in one.

So great was national pride in the temple that when Alexander
offered the entire loot from his Eastern campaign for the privilege of
inscribing his name in the place, they turned him down.

Ephesus took upon itself the humble-proud title *"Neocorus,"* the
Greek word for "temple sweeper," to symbolize its devotion to the
temple cult, and even inscribed the word boastfully on its coins.

Focal point for devotees inside the temple was the statue of Diana
or Artemis. ("Diana" is the Latin form for the Greek "Artemis.")
This statue was not the shapely Greek goddess we imagine, like the
tall, lovely figure of Diana, goddess of hunting, on display in the
Louvre. Ephesus' Diana or Artemis was disgustingly ugly. Resting on
a huge meteoric stone which had fallen eons earlier was a crude
wooden statue—a repulsive female fertility figure with enormous hips
and protruding belly, capped by rows of pendulant breasts.

The rites of worship associated with Artemis were unabashedly
erotic. The shrine was Big Business. Hundreds of thousands of visitors made pilgrimages to Ephesus. Such an atmosphere fostered the
proliferation of every cult, perversion, and superstition in the Orient.

Paul and his cohorts did not attack Ephesus head-on, but concentrated at first, as usual, on the Jewish colony. For three months, he
worked at the synagogue, ". . . arguing and pleading about the kingdom of God. . . ." (ACTS 19:8) Some of his hearers, however, were
"stubborn" (ACTS 19:9), or, literally, "hardened like gristle," and

forced Paul to withdraw. The church separated from the synagogue at Ephesus.

Ever resourceful, Paul borrowed the school hall of a teacher of rhetoric and philosophy named Tyrannus. During the siesta hour in the middle of the day when Tyrannus was not using his hall, Paul met with the new Christians. Paul worked each morning weaving tent cloth, then used the break during the hot part of the day, from 11:00 a.m. to 4:00 p.m. when most workers rested, to hold church meetings and classes.

After two years of such intensive effort, the church took deep root in the area of Ephesus. At the same time, Paul and his associates found themselves fighting a never-ending battle with superstition. Even Paul's sweat-cloths and workman's aprons were picked up from his bench and taken by superstitious Ephesians to the sick for their supposed therapeutic value!

Luke passed on an amusing tidbit of local gossip telling how one group of religious quacks had an incantation using the name of Jesus backfire. These particular itinerant exorcists were turncoat Jews, seven sons of a priest named Sceva. One day, while trying to heal a man with an evil spirit, the seven spiritual racketeers were challenged by the spirit. "Jesus, I know, and Paul I know;" the demon shrieked, "but who are you?" (ACTS 19:15) Suddenly, the sick man went berserk, ripping and clawing the seven so badly that they fled disheveled, bleeding, and disgraced into the street.

This episode made such a profound impression in Ephesus that Paul was given a hearing among many who took magic seriously. Paul's enemy at Ephesus was not sophisticated philosophy, as at Athens, but dark and deeply imbedded superstition.

The Ephesian "letters" were ancient monograms supposedly endowed with magical properties. Many people made a lifetime study of these inscriptions. Elaborate systems of mystical formularies were drawn up, each with its own powers at certain times and circumstances. There were so many various combinations of these "letters" that countless expensive scrolls or books were sold. Although a hodgepodge of numerology, astrology, and plain hocum, the books of black arts were taken with life-or-death seriousness at Ephesus. Many strange stories were told about the alleged effects of Ephesian magic.

Along with belief in magic went a frantic trust in charms, amulets, talismen, and other goodluck pieces. Fortunes were made peddling articles of junk to ward off evil spells.

Paul demonstrated so powerfully that the Holy Spirit is more powerful than the power of any sorcerer that many Ephesians were deeply affected. Some in the church had continued to dabble in the occult on the sly; these came ". . . confessing and divulging their practices." (ACTS 19:18) Others in Ephesus, convinced that no magic arts could compete with the Holy Spirit, renounced their trinkets and secret formulae. One night, at a great public gathering, disillusioned former magic practitioners threw some ten thousand dollars' worth of paraphernalia on a huge bonfire.

Perhaps we smile in a sophisticated way, thinking that this kind of undiluted superstition is something the human race has now left behind. Far from it!

Approximately thirty million Americans have varying degrees of faith in astrology. No one can estimate how much soothsayers, palm-readers, crystal-gazers, hex-chasers, and other gyps fleece from a gullible public. Astrologists alone collect one hundred million dollars annually, and few major U.S. newspapers dare omit the daily horoscope.

In the Orient today business ventures, governmental decisions, or personal plans are seldom considered without consulting the astrologers. Even western-educated professional people carefully carry charms. Belief in various demons and jinns is so strong that in Thailand a "spirit house"—something like an undersized dog house on a pole—is mounted in front of nearly every Thai house to keep the spirits out of the residence.

Some people mistakenly think that all the church must do is to show by rational proofs that such "spirits" do not exist and that astrology is unscientific. The truth is that few people are rational or logical in their thinking.

God did not hand down arguments to convince people of the folly of believing in black arts. Instead, the Holy Spirit asserted that He is stronger than any sorcery, more powerful than the grip of any magic, the spell of any spirit, the malice of any jinx! Writing to the church at Ephesus, Paul speaks matter-of-factly of the apparent reality of such malevolent spirits, and warns Christians to depend upon the Spirit's power ". . . against the principalities, against the powers, against the world rulers of this present darkness, against the spiritual hosts of wickedness in the heavenly places." (EPHESIANS 6:12)

Paul won the round against the practitioners of the black arts and made plans to move on. He had been in Ephesus two years. The church was well rooted.

151

Moody and mean, bigoted and boisterous, Ephesus, however, did not look favorably on the new group. The "Temple Sweeper" for great Diana, wanted a fanatic loyalty to its goddess. More serious, the decline of magic at Ephesus meant a decline in visitors. When the tourist trade fell off, business dropped—and one of the biggest businesses at Ephesus was the manufacture and sale of miniatures of Artemis.

Models of the goddess have turned up all over the Mediterranean world, showing how popular and widely circulated they were. These portable shrines were carried on trips, into battle, in devotional processions, and into private homes. Hundreds of thousands of these wooden, silver, or gold statues of Artemis were hawked at souvenir stands at Ephesus.

When the church's preaching began to hurt the shrine business, there was bound to be trouble. The powerful bloc of statue-makers, silversmiths, and master craftsmen called a meeting. Organized and conducted by a particularly hostile shrine-maker, Demetrius, the meeting dissolved into an irate, riot-bound mob.

Demetrius cleverly appealed to the group's piety, patriotism, and pocketbooks—all at the same time. The gospel was cutting into their business. What was bad for their business was bad for their national economy. What was bad for the economy was a slam at Ephesus. Any slur on Ephesus was an affront to Artemis herself. So Demetrius' argument ran. He climaxed his speech with high-octane oratory, shouting, "And there is danger not only that this trade of ours may come into disrepute but also that the temple of the great goddess Artemis may count for nothing, and that she may even be deposed from her magnificence, she whom all Asia and the world worship." (ACTS 19:27)

Demetrius' fears came true. Today, Ephesus is a silt-filled plain studded with ruins. Nothing whatsoever is left of the temple of Artemis. Only the sound of the wind soughing through the grass and the bleat of an occasional goat break the desolate stillness.

The speech, however, had an incendiary effect. The enraged silversmiths crashed out of the meeting and fomented a riot. After rampaging through the streets, the mob poured into the huge, 20,000-seat amphitheater to hold a mass rally and plan further mischief.

John Wesley, experienced with angry crowds, advised his early Methodist associates, "Always look a mob in the face." Paul, veteran of equally as many tumults, wanted to stand up to the Ephesian mob that day. He was prevented by some of the disciples, but two others of his party, Gaius and Aristarchus, were seized.

After several hours of confusion and shouting in the amphitheater, the crowd finally grudgingly listened to the town clerk, the top civic official who acted as go-between for the city government and Rome. The town clerk soothed the crowd with platitudes about Artemis' greatness and her cult's universality, pointed out the legal channels through which grievances should be taken, and advised the crowd to break up and go home before there were charges of civil disorder— smoothly hinting of Rome's possible displeasure.

Whenever the gospel touches any vested interests, there is bound to be an uproar. Men still try to put a halo around their purse and their flag.

The Spirit-filled church is an old hand at provoking riots. Don't for a moment think that its task is to avoid upsetting people or to protect the status quo. Instead, the Holy Spirit still threatens man's sanctified self-interest. Every parish, if the Spirit is at work, will be a little Ephesus from time to time.

Even before the Ephesus riot, Paul had ". . . resolved in the Spirit to pass through Macedonia and Achaia and go to Jerusalem, saying, 'After I have been there, I must also see Rome.'" (ACTS: 19:21) Led by the Spirit, Paul planned to re-visit the string of congregations he had left behind at Philippi, Thessalonica, Beroea, Corinth, and the areas adjacent to each of these centers.

It was to be more than a social visit. Knowing the acute distress of many in the Jerusalem church, Paul dreamed of collecting a special offering. Such an offering would unite all the Gentile congregations in one act of compassion. It would also demonstrate the unity of the church everywhere, illustrating that when one member of the Body suffers, all suffer. Paul hoped, furthermore, that each congregation would also send one of its number to help deliver the special collection in person. After successfully delivering the relief fund, Paul had general plans to visit Rome and strengthen the believers there.

Accompanied by Tychicus and Trophimus, trusted associates from Ephesus, Paul arrived at Philippi, where they were rejoined by Timothy and Erastus. Shoring up the leadership in the various congregations in Philippi, Thessalonica, and Beroea, the group even traveled over to the west coast to Illyricum to evangelize (see ROMANS 15:19).

Meanwhile, Paul was working to collect the relief fund. Each congregation was urged to contribute both money and a representative to personalize the concern. As Paul's party moved south into Greece, it gradually grew larger as it collected members of the deputation to Jerusalem.

Instead of a pleasant reunion with his Corinthian converts, however, Paul tumbled into an ant-hill of scorn and criticism. From II Corinthians, we learn that Paul spent a miserable three months among that congregation. Furthermore, in volatile Corinth, there were enemies in the synagogue who had not forgiven him for his work on his earlier visit. Just before the entire delegation of representatives was ready to sail from Corinth on the first leg of the trip to Jerusalem, Paul got wind of a plot. Knowing how easy it would be to kill him on a crowded pilgrim ship, Paul changed plans at the last minute. The two Ephesian members of the party, Tychicus and Trophimus, sailed as planned, promising to wait for Paul at Troas, and Paul and the others raced north to Philippi.

We barely notice, as we read this section of Acts, that the "we" sections have resumed, indicating that Luke joined the party again at Philippi. For the rest of the narrative we have the account of an eyewitness and personal participant.

Paul was a wanted man by this time in most of the brawling Greek-speaking world. Hounded by a sort of Ku Klux Klan of synagogue fanatics, Paul sensed that he would not be able to work openly and unmolested any longer in the eastern Mediterranean. In fact, he began to have intimations that a conspiracy might eventually take his life. He confessed that by the time he crossed to Troas, ". . . we felt we had received the sentence of death. . . ." (II CORINTHIANS 1:9) For these reasons, Paul was more anxious than ever to hurry his delegation from the Gentile congregations with their special offerings to Jerusalem. Time was showing signs of running out. An ominous note of foreboding crept into Paul's speeches. The trip to Jerusalem took on the markings of a farewell tour.

Like an old doctor chuckling over an amusing case, Luke interrupts his narrative to tell us about a near-tragedy at Troas which everyone laughed about later. Groggy from the odor of the lamps, the heat of the crowd, and the lateness of the hour (and perhaps also by the length of Paul's sermon), a young man named Eutychus, perched on the window ledge, fell asleep and plummeted to the ground three stories below. To everyone's relief, the boy, although knocked out briefly, was unhurt.

Returning to his narrative, Luke, like an experienced mariner with his finger on the chart, meticulously indicates the route and the stops from Troas to Caesarea. At Miletus, the port for Ephesus, Paul had a final meeting with the leaders of the Ephesian church. It was an emotion-packed reunion, for Paul bluntly acknowledged, ". . . I am going to Jerusalem, bound in the Spirit, not knowing what shall befall me there; except that the Holy Spirit testifies to me in every city that imprisonment and afflictions await me." (ACTS 20:22-23)

Although it was Paul's farewell address to the Gentile branch of the church which he had loved and served so much, there was no self-pity. Matter-of-factly, Paul reminded everyone how he had earned his own livelihood, answering the smears that he had preached to line his own pockets. He concluded, "And now I commend you to God . . ." (ACTS 20:32) using the Greek term for making a deposit at a bank. His Gentile converts were his only wealth or "savings"! Quoting words of Jesus which are not found anywhere else in the New Testament, Paul added, "It is more blessed to give than to receive." (ACTS 20:35)

Warning the inexperienced leaders of a congregation of recent converts from raw paganism who were immersed in a city full of the allurements of their former life, Paul soberly advised, "Take heed to yourselves and to all the flock, in which the Holy Spirit has made you guardians, to feed the church of the Lord . . . I know that after my departure fierce wolves will come in among you . . . and from among your own selves will arise men speaking perverse things, to draw away disciples. . . ." (ACTS 20:28-30)

"You . . . will see my face no more," (ACTS 20:25) Paul warned. Although the Ephesians never saw Paul's face again, he continued to stand with them. Through letters, prayers, and personal emissaries, Paul did all he could to strengthen and encourage Ephesus and his other children.

Paul realized what we sometimes overlook: where the church is a puny minority in a hostile culture, it needs the support of those of the church elsewhere. In a country such as Japan, for instance, where only about one out of every two hundred is a Christian, the church in the rest of the world must constantly remember the church in Japan in its giving and in its praying.

Paul knew that no path of ease lay ahead, but prison, trouble, torture, and death. To him the important thing was not how successful he was, how long he lived, or how comfortable he became. "But I do not account my life of any value nor as precious to myself," Paul affirmed, "if only I may accomplish my course and the ministry which I received from the Lord Jesus, to testify to the gospel of the grace of God." (ACTS 20:24) Life's purpose, to the Apostle to the Gentiles, was to be faithful to Jesus Christ. Trusting in Him through the Holy Spirit, Paul knew that he could face the bleakest tomorrow.

22

COURAGE BORN OF CONVICTION

(ACTS 21:1 - 23:11)

"YOU WILL SEE MY FACE NO MORE," PAUL TOLD THE EPHESIAN elders.

The closer Paul came to Jerusalem, the more it became obvious that his fears were well founded. At each port of call, the more insistent the storm warnings became. At Tyre, "through the Spirit, they told Paul not to go on to Jerusalem." (ACTS 21:4) At Caesarea, a Christian prophet named Agabus, taking a leaf from his Old Testament counterparts, tried to dissuade Paul, dramatically tying Paul's hands and feet to symbolize what would befall him at Jerusalem. Even Luke begged Paul not to risk his life this way. At Caesarea, the last stop before Jerusalem, Paul's friends broke down and cried, pointing out the dangers in continuing.

Should Paul have gone to Jerusalem? Who was right, Paul or the countless friends who pleaded with him not to go?

Much as Paul realized the gravity of going up to Jerusalem, much as he appreciated the affectionate concern of everyone in the church —even those in Palestine with whom he had once violently disagreed—Paul would not be talked out of his plans.

The Jerusalem church was like a beseiged garrison, alone and cut off from supplies, beleaguered for so long that it was fatigued and uncertain. Famine and persecution had ground it down, blunting its aggressiveness. Far from carrying the gospel to the street corners, the church had retreated defensively, maintaining a holding operation.

Sensitive to its fears and needs and resolved to pump new vigor into the disciples at the capital, Paul collected his party for the last lap. The special offering and visitors from the far-flung Gentile congregations would be living proof of the one-ness of the Body of Christ. What more positive evidence could Jerusalem Christians ever have of the support and love of Christian brothers everywhere? What

157

better way to remind the Jerusalem congregation that the Holy Spirit still acted?

The sacrificial thing to do is not necessarily the sensible. Proper though it was for Christians to be concerned about Paul's safety, Paul knew that it was more important to be obedient to the living Jesus Christ.

Lodging at Jerusalem with Mnason, an early disciple, Paul and his party received a genuine welcome, typical of the hospitality that members of the early church showed toward one another (something which we could well emulate!). "When we had come to Jerusalem," Luke writes, "the brethren received us gladly." (ACTS 21:17)

The Gentile delegation presented the special relief fund collected from the distant Greek and Asian congregations, and Paul reported in detail ". . . the things that God had done among the Gentiles through his ministry." (ACTS 21:19)

Although thankful for the help of Paul's party and grateful for the Spirit's witness in the Gentile world, the Jerusalem Christians were somber. Paul, they reported, had the reputation of being Judaism's arch subversive, and Jerusalem was boiling with lies and rumors about Paul's teachings. When word got around that Paul was in town—as it most certainly would—they grimly warned that anything might happen.

To protect Paul and to refute the smears, the Jerusalem believers insisted that Paul take a temporary Jewish Nazarite vow with four others. An ancient custom mentioned in Numbers 6, whereby a man did not shave or cut his hair or drink wine, the Nazarite vow became a custom among Jews who, having come through some peril, wanted to testify publicly that God had delivered them. In Paul's day, the long ceremonial had been shortened to thirty days, after which the hair would be shaved and burned on the temple altar with suitable offerings.

The Jerusalem brethren seemed to be led more by expediency at this point than by the Spirit. Curiously, there is no mention of prayer, no word of what the Spirit wished. About the most that can be said for the Nazarite vow plan is that it reflected an honest desire to look after Paul. Practically speaking, Paul's appearing as a Nazarite would be public refutation of the charges that he was an iconoclastic libertine out to shred temple ceremonial.

Perhaps Paul agreed that it would be good public relations. Possibly he thought that he would have to demonstrate dramatically that he did not disparage the law. Probably Paul, anxious to be as cooperative and conciliatory as possible, with inner misgivings subjected himself to his brethren. Paul had often spoken of the mutual responsibility of members of the Body, the church, to one another. At Jerusalem, Paul faced a practical application of what he had preached as to whether he believed the Christian community had a responsibility to a church member and whether the church member had a responsibility to heed the admonition of the Christian community. After the circumcision controversy, Paul was anxious to keep harmony, especially with the Jerusalem church.

Regardless of Paul's inner thoughts or motives, the Nazarite vow was a throwback to legalism, a bow to ceremonial—the very thing that Paul had so strenuously opposed. Like all compromises, it was supported by pragmatic reasons. Was this scheme of the Jerusalem believers, practical though it seemed, inspired by the Spirit?

Paying the expenses of the vow for four poor Jerusalem Christians, as suggested, Paul appeared in the temple to begin the ceremony. Seven days after the time period had begun, as was customary, Paul went back to the temple to notify the priests of the date when his four poor associates and he would complete the vow and present their offerings.

Meanwhile, in tinderbox Jerusalem, more emotionally incendiary than ever with thousands of hot-eyed pilgrims crowding in for the Feast of Pentecost, news had been passed that Paul was in town.

Fanatics from Ephesus spotted a home-town man, Trophimus, on the Jerusalem streets with Paul. Perhaps someone from the pilgrim ships had detected other Gentiles in Paul's party.

Paul would never have been so fool-hardy as to try to smuggle Trophimus or any other Gentile into the temple. At the foot of the steps leading to the inner court was a railing with a prominent inscription in Greek and Latin warning any uncircumcised person not to trespass on pain of immediate death. Paul, who had been a teacher of the law, a resident at Jerusalem, and worshipper at the temple for years, knew that any Gentile caught beyond the Court of the Women would be slaughtered on the spot, no questions asked. Nonetheless, the rumor suddenly cycloned through the crowds that Paul had taken Trophimus into the temple!

Paul was coming through the temple after giving the priest the week's notice about the termination of the vow. Someone screamed that Paul had desecrated the holy place, igniting the excitable bystanders. Suddenly frenzied, they surged around Paul and he collapsed under a deluge of punches and kicks. The temple guards

159

shoved the shrieking mass outside the temple area so that Paul's death would not pollute the sacred place. To prevent Paul from rushing inside for sanctuary in case he should break loose, the guards clanged shut the great gates.

High in the Tower of Antonia, the Roman fort looming over the temple area, a lookout noticed the uproar and shouted the alarm. Always at Red Alert during tense Jewish holidays, a tough, riot-control squad sprinted from action stations, wading into the crowd with staves swinging.

The commanding officer, a hard-bitten tribune of the cohort named Claudius Lysias, clapped Paul into chains, assuming Paul was a fiery Egyptian rebel and assassin who was the current Roman army headache. He tried to get facts, but dozens of furious screamers, all accusing the prisoner simultaneously, made any interrogation impossible. Grim-faced, the tribune ordered his men to pick up the prisoner and carry him into the barracks to keep him from being ripped from their grip by the tugging, shrieking mob.

Paul startled the tribune by addressing him in Greek, assuring him in a brief exchange shouted above the uproar that he was no Egyptian revolutionary but a Jew. ". . . I beg you," Paul called, "let me speak to the people." (ACTS 21:39) Hoping that his prisoner might calm the mob and persuade it to disperse, Lysias agreed.

Speaking loudly in the Palestinian dialect, Paul finally quieted the crowd.

"I am a Jew," he announced, "born at Tarsus in Cilicia, but brought up in this city at the feet of Gamaliel, educated according to the strict manner of the law of our fathers, being zealous for God as you all are this day." (ACTS 22:3)

It was an excellent beginning. Paul made immediate contact with every listener. The assembly was hushed, willing to hear more from a man who from the age of thirteen had been trained as a teacher of the law and had had such close association with the holy city.

With disarming frankness, Paul told the crowd of his past as a fanatic in the Old Testament tradition. Without embellishing and without hiding the facts, he acknowledged his record as a persecuter of Christians. Possibly there were some present who recalled Paul's participation in Stephen's execution.

Paul moved on to his experience on the road to Damascus, giving great credit to Ananias. Using Ananias' reputation as a good Jew to enhance his own case, Paul referred to him as a "devout man according to the law, well-spoken of by all the Jews. . . ." (ACTS 22:12)

To underscore how deeply rooted in Jewish practice and how authentic his commission by the Lord was, Paul said that it came during the time he was actually praying in the temple. Far from destroying or profaning the temple, Paul implied, he traced his entire career to an experience in the temple. It was there that Jesus Christ instructed Paul, "I will send you far away to the Gentiles."

GENTILES!! Paul pressed the red button and the crowd exploded. Such xenophobic hatred toward the uncircumcised was mass paranoia. The mob had listened with indifference to Paul's conversion account, with apathy to the claims for Jesus Christ, but mere mention of anyone going to Gentiles ignited uncontrollable rage!

"Up to this word they listened to him; then they lifted up their voices and said, 'Away with such a fellow from the earth! For he ought not to live.'" (ACTS 22:22) Completely losing any shred of orderliness, inflamed by shrill, hate-filled voices urging death to Paul, the crowd erupted into leaderless rabble.

It was hopeless to argue or even to be heard. Nervous that the furor was getting out of hand, the tribune had Paul yanked inside the barracks.

The officer barked an order. The centurion quickly stripped, stretched, and tied Paul, preparing to work him over with a scourging to learn the truth. Scourging, a brutal lashing with metal-tipped cat-o-nine tails, could mean being crippled or killed, was so deadly it was reserved for slaves and prisoners, could never be done to a Roman citizen. Paul revealed that he was a Roman citizen, and flustered, the centurion called for the tribune, Lysias. Flogging Romans was inviting court-martial, and the agitated tribune cross-examined Paul. Both he and Paul knew that Paul would not dare make such a claim unless he could verify it, because the penalty for pretending to be a Roman citizen was death.

Not quite certain what to do with Paul, the nervous tribune kept him overnight, the following day summoning the priests and the council to hear their charges against the prisoner.

Paul opened his defense, "Brethren." He had no animosity toward his accusers; he still considered himself as good a Jew as any of them.

"I have lived," he continued, "before God in all good conscience up to this day." (ACTS 23:1) His words, however, were interpreted as blasphemy by the high priest. Enraged, the high priest gave an illegal command—Paul was cracked across the mouth.

Knowing that physical violence against a defendant patently violated all the rules of Jewish jurisprudence, Paul flared, "God shall strike you, you whitewashed wall! Are you sitting to judge me according to the law, and yet contrary to the law you order me to be struck?" (ACTS 23:3)

Self-righteously indignant, other Council members informed Paul that his blast had been aimed at the high priest. Paul, quickly getting control of himself and remembering his court procedure, apologized for any discourtesy shown, claiming that he had no way of telling it was the high priest.

Seizing the initiative and working the strategy of divide-and-conquer, Paul skillfully played on the rivalry simmering between the Pharisees and the Saducees among his accusers. He directed his appeal to brother Pharisees, pleading, "Brethren, I am a Pharisee, a son of Pharisees; with respect to the hope and the resurrection of the dead I am on trial." (ACTS 23:6) Paul was not hiding his convictions or sailing under false colors to save his skin. In good conscience, he could still call himself one of "the pious ones," a Pharisee, and because of Jesus Christ, he believed in the resurrection of the dead as never before. The long-standing feud over the resurrection between the Pharisees and the Sadducees burst. With many Pharisees shouting, "We find nothing wrong in this man . . ." (ACTS 23:9) the hearing ended in a near-brawl.

Roman tribunes did not scare easily, but Lysias feared for his prisoner's life. He ordered his men to remove Paul from the hearing-place because he was afraid that Paul would "be torn in pieces," literally, in the Greek, ripped apart as wild dogs tear a carcass or beasts dismember their prey.

After such a twenty-four-hour emotional and physical ordeal, Paul was weak, exhausted, and depressed. Alone in a Roman cell, threatened by violence and death, he felt isolated from friends, perhaps forgotten by God.

Everyone who has ever been in prison has commented on the desperate need for a friend. Marie Torre, the news reporter jailed for refusing to divulge information told her in confidence, vividly describes the melancholy and loneliness of prison (*Don't Quote Me*): "Everyone has to believe someone cares for her," she writes. "I don't think prisoners could retain their sanity otherwise. But the more I heard an inmate insist that someone 'really loves me,' the less likely it seemed to be true. There was sometimes a hint of panic in their voices. It sounded as though they were really trying to convince themselves, and it was not easy to listen to them."

There was no such self-deception with Paul, no desperate "some-one loves me." Luke say simply, "The following night the Lord stood by him. . . ." (ACTS 23:11) Through the Holy Spirit, Paul knew that Jesus keeps His word not to desert His own. "I will not leave you desolate; I will come to you," He assured His disciples before He was crucified (JOHN 14:18), and through the Spirit that night Paul was aware that Jesus fulfills His promise.

"Take courage," He told Paul (ACTS 23:11), using the identical Greek word used to cheer the paralytic (MATTHEW 9:2), the hemor-rhaging woman (MATTHEW 9:22), the blind man (MARK 10:49), the disciples in the boat during the storm (MATTHEW 14:27), the discouraged disciples at the Last Supper (JOHN 16:33), a word with rich associations. Paul remembered how Jesus' "Take courage" had strengthened the resolve of others seized by depression, tempted to give up. With the Lord standing by him, Paul knew that he could face all things.

There will be times for us all when life will seem meaningless. We may cry for some sense or order in our personal existence. Conditions will be unstable; the outlook will be far from ideal. We may be ready to agree with Siegfried Sassoon, who, bitter from his experiences in the trenches wrote, "In 1917, I was only beginning to learn that life, for the majority of the population, is an unlovely struggle against unfair odds, culminating in a cheap funeral."

Not as ivory-tower theory but as Jerusalem-jail certainty, Paul could write, ". . . I am sure that neither death, nor life, nor angels, nor principalities, nor things present, nor things to come, nor powers, nor height, nor depth, nor anything else in all creation, will be able to separate us from the love of God in Christ Jesus our Lord." (ROMANS 8:38-39)

The Living Lord gave Paul not only encouragement but a promise: ". . . you must bear witness at Rome." (ACTS 23:11)

He blesses us with tranquility in the midst of storm, with strength in our weakness, with a future in the face of hopelessness, with responsibility in the midst of futility!

23

"WHO DARES, WINS!"

(ACTS 23:12 - 25:12)

TWO YEARS IS A BIG BLOCK OF TIME IN A MAN'S LIFETIME, ESPE-
cially if that man is burning with eagerness to accomplish something.

Plotted against, kept in custody, Paul sat through two years of
discouragement and frustration when every plan was thwarted. Paul
was reminded again that trust in the gospel does not buy immunity
from problems or disappointment.

At least the period was not dull. Jerusalem's religious leaders were
persistently and frenziedly inciting Judea into a shrieking orgy of hate
which ended with a Gotterdämmerung-like finale some fifteen years
later in the blood and burning of a suicidal revolt against Rome.

Typical of the Judean insanity was the plot to murder Paul. Simple
and sinister as a dagger thrust, the plan was to ask the tribune to have
Paul brought from the barracks for another hearing. While Paul and
his few guards would be enroute, a crew of assassins would strike,
dispatch Paul, and melt into the crowds. The operation would finish
off Paul, implicate no one and take only five minutes.

The conspirators, ready to resort to any violence, bound themselves by a blood oath, swearing to God that they would get Paul or
else, thus trying to make God party to a murder plot! The entire
scheme was hatched with the approval of the temple authorities,
showing to what depths Jerusalem had sunk. The high priest and his
henchmen openly connived to kill Paul.

Paul's life was saved when his nephew somehow picked up rumors
of the plot and ran to the Roman barracks to warn him. Paul heard of
the plot and sent his nephew on to the tribune. Who was this nephew?
A student at Jerusalem, or a visitor in town? How did he hear
of the plot? What ultimately became of him?

We are tantalized by dozens of unanswered questions about this
sudden addition to Luke's cast of characters. From the tone used by

the Roman tribune and by the fact the tribune took his hand, we surmise that he was a youngster. It is obvious, too, that courage was a family trait in Paul's line; it was no small thing for a boy in Jerusalem to march alone up to the Roman barracks and spill details of an assassination plot, knowing the reprisals that could be exacted against him or his family.

Determined to outfox the plotters, Lysias took immediate steps to get Paul out of reach of any would-be assassins. Seventy cavalrymen and two hundred infantrymen, enough to handle any local crew of cutthroats, escorted Paul out of Jerusalem after dark about nine o'clock that night. The infantrymen accompanied the party as far as the watering place of Antipatris at the foot of the tortuous mountain road, halfway to Caesarea and safely past the danger zone. Paul and the horse guards arrived at Caesarea at daybreak after an all-night ride.

The party reported to Felix, the governor or procurator, handing him a letter-report from Lysias. Somehow, Luke got his hands on a copy of this letter, perhaps from seeing the original or from hearing it read many times or from borrowing a copy given Paul as prisoner, and he shares it with readers of Acts.

With typical military terseness, Lysias' letter states that he is passing on Paul to Felix for safety, but adds specifically that Paul is ". . . charged with nothing deserving death or imprisonment." (ACTS 23:29)

At the same time, Lysias the tribune, careful to cover himself against all possible criticism (a trait noticeable in nearly every military report ever written!), says nothing about mistakenly identifying Paul as the Egyptian revolutionary, or arresting Paul so hastily, or almost nearly scourging a Roman citizen. Strictly speaking, Lysias was on shaky legal ground.

Felix, the governor, detained Paul in a guard room in Herod's cavernous fortress until his accusers could present charges. Roman governors, especially in roiling eastern provinces, won nods from the home office at Rome by keeping the peace, and Felix was taking no chances that Paul or anyone else would disturb things. Already in hot water at Rome for abuses of office, Felix did not care if Paul's case never came to trial.

But it was only a matter of days until the hornet-angry accusers turned up at Caesarea. The deputation from the temple, headed by Ananias the high priest, had gone to the trouble to hire an Italian professional case-pleader named Tertellus.

Tertellus, with the oily self-assurance of a man who knows his way around court houses and enjoys strutting before the nervous provincials, opened his presentation with flourishes of heavy flattery; "Since through you we enjoy much peace, and since by your provision, most excellent Felix, reforms are introduced on behalf of this nation, in every way and everywhere we accept this with all gratitude." (ACTS 24:2-3)

Even Felix must have smiled. Notoriously corrupt and brutal, this scheming martinet was loathed by the Jews and allowed to continue in office only by the intervention of his brother Pallas, one of the Emperor's cronies.

Tertellus smoothly continued by making insinuations about Paul's life and actions, all unprovable, all defamatory. With lip-curling derision, Tertellus called Paul ". . . a pestilent fellow, an agitator among all the Jews throughout the world, and a ringleader of the sect of the Nazarenes." (ACTS 24:5) The closest Tertellus came to any specific accusation was to charge that Paul ". . . even tried to profane the temple. . . ." (ACTS 24:6) Implying that his clients legally arrested Paul, Tertellus added, "But we seized him." (ACTS 24:6) In many early manuscripts, there is an additional verse, "But the chief captain Lysias came and with great violence took him out of our hands," (ACTS 24:7 in footnote of RSV) showing how completely Tertellus distorted the facts.

Felix motioned for Paul to reply. Rising to make his own defense, Paul had no Tertellus, no profesional pleader, at his side. Paul's only helper was the Holy Spirit, and it is significant that one of the words for the Spirit in the New Testament is the Greek word *parakletes,* meaning literally "one who pleads another's cause" or advisor, counselor, and helper.

Courteous, yet refusing to use sticky adulation, Paul replied. He calmly refuted the smears, point by point, by laying out the facts. Stating that it was only twelve days since he had arrived at Jerusalem, he said that he came to worship, not to agitate, patiently explaining his actions in terms a Roman could understand. Paul's defense then went on to show that the entire hearing was out of order. His accusers, Asian Jews, were not present as they should have been. There was no proof of any of the charges. Without resorting to name-calling, Paul made it clear that Rome's officials in Judea were not following Roman procedure.

"But this I admit to you," Paul soberly stated, "that according to the Way, which they call a sect, I worship the God of our fathers. . . ." (ACTS 24:13) Here is the crux of the disagreement. Is the gospel of Jesus Christ "the Way" or "a sect"? Is the cross and resurrection *the* road of salvation, or merely the silly, obnoxious tenet of a silly, obnoxious ism?

Wily Felix, ". . . having a rather accurate knowledge of the Way. . . ." (ACTS 24:22), had already checked up on the Christian church and should have released Paul immediately. Instead, he announced that he would defer judgment until Lysias appeared. This shrewd move got the temple leaders out of Felix's hair without antagonizing them.

Although conditions were eased somewhat—the chains were removed, visitors were permitted—Paul was still a prisoner.

Felix, however, was curious about his prisoner. With his wife, Drusilla, he turned up asking to be entertained by a sermon. Paul refused to put on a pulpit show. Instead, he ". . . argued about justice and self-control and future judgment. . . ." (ACTS 24:25) This hit Felix where it hurt: *Justice* (Felix had once hired killers to replace Jonathan, a critical high priest); *Self-control* (Felix had seduced Drusilla while she was married to another). Not surprisingly, Felix was alarmed and cried, "Go away for the present; when I have an opportunity, I will summon you." (ACTS 24:25)

At the same time, Felix hoped that a deal might be worked out with Paul, knowing that the prisoner had friends and access to money. Felix let it be known that the right sum could quietly and speedily get Paul acquitted.

Was Paul tempted to go along with Felix's offer?

The insidious thing about temptation is that it is always plausible, can even be masked under the cover of "goodness." A number of strong reasons for slipping money to Felix presented themselves: Paul could have gone on with his travels; the churches needed to be strengthened; Paul had already wasted precious weeks; he had a good chance of lingering permanently behind bars.

Paul refused to buy himself an acquital by selling his principles. Regardless of the pseudonym that Felix's scheme used, its real name was bribery. Expedient though it might have been to give money to Felix, Paul steadfastly remembered his responsibility as a Christian.

Meanwhile, Paul's stay in the Caesarea cellblock extended from weeks into months . . . into one year . . . into two years.

Shielded by his brother Pallas, one of Nero's sycophants, Felix managed to hang on for years as procurator of Judea. Eventually, even Pallas' influence could not offset Felix's record of corruption and cruelty, and he was recalled to Rome.

It was customary for departing governors to turn loose anyone in prisons as a parting gesture of good will. Paul, remembering this practice, undoubtedly let his hopes rise.

Felix, aware of the Jewish charges waiting for him at Rome and afraid of further damaging reports, decided to let Paul languish in prison.

The man who had the misfortune to be Felix's successor was a brisk, honest administrator who would have made a good name for himself anywhere but in Judea. Festus, the new procurator, found everything stacked against him. His predecessors' high-handed incompetency in handling the Jews had left a legacy of profound hate and truculence toward all Romans.

On Festus' initial visit to Jerusalem, the temple authorities, dusting off the old plot to kill Paul which was foiled by the tribune Lysias, asked that Paul be brought back to Jerusalem to stand trial. Suspecting the Jerusalem religious leaders of chicanery, yet wanting to get off to a good start with them, Festus stalled. ". . . let the men of authority among you go down with me," Festus parried, "and if there is anything wrong about the man, let them accuse him." (ACTS 25:5)

The hearing before Festus at Caesarea was another pointless round, the same "serious charges which they could not prove." (ACTS 25:7) To the perplexed Festus, it was a deadlock between shrill you-did-so accusers and a calm I-did-not defendant. Whom to believe? How to get to the bottom of this case? As a new man, Festus was understandably bewildered and irritated by this bit of unfinished business which Felix had left on his desk.

Anxious not to rile the touchy temple leaders, Festus tried to be conciliatory. Perhaps their original suggestion to have Paul tried on religious charges at Jerusalem, Festus mused, was not so bad after all. Turning to Paul, Festus blandly asked, "Do you wish to go up to Jerusalem and there be tried on these charges before me?" (ACTS 25:9)

Paul was both appalled and annoyed at Festus' naivety. First of all, Paul knew that his adversaries would not hesitate to ambush him. Secondly, Paul knew that if Festus did release him to the Sanhedrin, he was as good as dead. Paul saw the booby traps in the temple leaders' proposal.

Paul was further incensed that Roman justice had mired down so completely. There were absolutely no Roman charges involved in Paul's case, and the religious charges, which had no place in a Roman court, were flimsy and unsupported.

Paul saw that he was getting nowhere at Caesarea. Trapped in the snakepit of intrigue, weary of the machinations of provincial politics, he knew that he still held one trump card. In spite of the implied slur against Festus' impartiality, Paul stood on his rights as a Roman citizen. "I APPEAL TO CAESAR!" (ACTS 25:11) he announced.

The case was instantly shifted to Rome. Nothing could stop Paul's appeal. He was irrevocably committed.

In a sense, it was probably a relief to be cut loose from the stringy suspicions and accusations which had been clinging to him for two years. Also, it was undoubtedly exhilarating for Paul to realize that, at last, he would see Rome.

At the same time, it was a calculated risk. "I appeal to Caesar!" was a good law, but "Caesar" in this case was a murdering maniac named Nero. An Emperor who could casually order his own mother, his stepbrother, and his wife killed could hardly be trusted to have much interest in the life of an obscure citizen from Tarsus.

But Paul understood that, in a sense, all of life is a risk. Day by day, whether he was called upon to face Nero at Rome, a mob on the streets, a congregation in a synagogue, or the walls of the Caesarea cellblock, he dared take the risk of being Jesus Christ's ambassador.

Jesus took *the* risk—risked everything for us at the cross. On Easter, we know for a certainty that He won! He tells us we, too, can risk anything in His service because the victory is assured!

In World War II, a bold, brainy young Scotsman in the British Army, Captain David Stirling, planned and trained a special striking force operating deep behind enemy lines which prepared the way for Allied victory in North Africa. The motto of this elite company was, "Who Dares, Wins."

We can dare because we know God has already won! The Holy Spirit, re-presenting the news of the manger, the cross, and the resurrection to us, empowers us to take the calculated risk of meeting the challenge of any Nero. With the Spirit, who dares, wins!

24

VALEDICTORY IN CHAINS

(ACTS 25:13 - 26:32)

LIKE BEING LOCKED TO A CONVEYER BELT, PAUL'S APPEAL TO CAESAR meant being carried to Rome. The wheel of justice, once in motion, could not possibly be stopped or reversed.

As far as Festus was concerned, Paul's case was now transferred to the Emperor. All that Festus had to do was to prepare a report to send to Rome with the prisoner. The only problem was, what should he write? Festus had no concrete accusation against Paul.

At this point, Agrippa, local vassal king under the Romans, turned up at Caesarea for a ceremonial visit to extend his official welcome to Festus.

Agrippa had descended from an infamous family: his father, Herod Agrippa, had beheaded James and imprisoned Peter; his great grandfather had slaughtered the babies at Bethlehem; his great uncle had executed John the Baptist. Agrippa, in spite of his Jewish blood, had outraged public opinion by marrying his own sister and offended pious Jews by building his palace to overlook the temple. The title "king," given by Rome because he was a pliable toady, made Agrippa something like a raj in India during the British heyday, permitting him a few harmless privileges such as picking the high priests and governing the temple. He abused even these privileges, however, by continually reshuffling the priests in the temple.

To Festus, both Paul's position and that of the fanatic Jews were parts of a strange, senseless cult. ". . . They had certain points of dispute with him," Festus said, "about their own superstition and about one Jesus, who was dead, but whom Paul asserted to be alive." (ACTS 25:19)

Bewildered by the apparent squabble over subtle points, Festus asked Agrippa's advice. Festus recognized that Agrippa had a hat-tipping relationship to Israel's faith and yet was Romanized enough to be neutral to its promises.

Agrippa, ever anxious for an interesting diversion, said, "I should like to hear the man myself," much as he would have asked to listen to an amusing comedian or watch a clever juggler.

With all the pomp and strutting that typified an Oriental court, Agrippa and the leading citizens of Caesarea gathered the following day to hear Paul. After listening to a quick synopsis of Paul's arrest and previous hearings by Festus, Agrippa signaled Paul to begin.

Martin Niemöller, the German Christian arrested by the Nazis and subjected to nearly nine years of prison horrors, made a speaking tour of American churches shortly after World War II. Two newspaper reporters were overheard discussing Niemöller's address in one city. "Imagine!" muttered one reporter disgustedly, "Nine years in a Nazi prison and all he can talk about is Jesus Christ!"

Two years in a Caesarea cell and all Paul could talk about was Jesus Christ! He did not sensationalize his experiences; he did not protest his innocence. In the third, final, and most complete presentation of Paul's conversion experience in Acts, Paul testified about the King to a king. Not particularly concerned about his future or his rights or his safety, Paul was most anxious to proclaim Jesus Christ.

Luke includes this long speech by Paul before Agrippa as a summary of how the Holy Spirit had been working to carry the Good News of Jesus Christ to outsiders as well as Jews. Dramatic though the scene was with Paul in manacles before a supercilious king, both Luke and Paul would focus our attention on the Spirit Himself. As Paul concluded, referring to the constant presence and activity of the Holy Spirit, "To this day, I have had the help that comes from God. . . ." (ACTS 26:22) Center stage front throughout this chapter is the Spirit, not Paul. Although Paul is the narrator and participant, the story is actually a capsule account of the Spirit's presenting the gospel to Gentiles.

Paul eloquently testified how the Spirit had introduced Jesus Christ as the Risen Lord to *him,* the one-time super-Jew and arch-foe of Christians.

There was an old proverb in the Greek classics about a rebellious young ox, learning the discipline of working in the traces. Hanging just behind the rambunctious animal was a goad, a heavy beam into which sharp wood prongs had been inserted. The harder the ox kicked the goad, the more it hurt. Finally, the ox learned to work quietly in harness and obey its master.

"Saul, Saul, why do you persecute me? It hurts you to kick against the goads," Paul reported Jesus saying to him in ACTS 26:14. Reminding his listeners of the proverb, Paul candidly stated that Jesus, his master, had to "break" him of rebelliousness and train him to a yoke of service.

To swaggering, conceited Agrippa, Paul's words seemed both amusing and disturbing. In spite of the chains, it began to appear that Paul was really free and Agrippa, actually a prisoner. Paul was enthroned; Agrippa, enslaved.

Paul knew that Jesus had brought him a new name, a new career, a new purpose, a new direction, a new life. Jesus had brought all these in bringing Himself.

"Who are you, Lord?" Paul remembered himself whispering. "And the Lord said, 'I am Jesus. . . .' " (ACTS 26:15) Jesus came not bringing a new philosophy, a new cult, a new ceremony, a new law. The hitherto-seemingly distant Lord came in person. All that is new was embodied in Him. Paul henceforth committed himself not to a new idea, not to a new religion, not to a new ethic, but to Jesus Christ.

Paul deliberately skipped most of the intimate personal details of his Damascus road experience, refusing to entertain with a sensational account. The essential fact was that Jesus Christ was not dead but alive.

A class of youngsters in a Christian school in Korea was drawing colored illustrations of Bible stories. One child, portraying his version of the healing of a sick man, startled the teacher by coloring the figure of Jesus' face, hands and clothes a brilliant green, while leaving the sick man a plain white. Puzzled by the unusual colors, the teacher asked the child for an explanation. To the child, it was obvious. Green meant life, as with trees and grass, and because Jesus is full of creative, life-giving power, the child associated green with Jesus. White, on the other hand, meant an absence of life. "Jesus," the boy explained, pointing to his picture, "is coming to give this sick man new life."

Paul, who would have understood the green Jesus, remembered the Lord had ordered him to ". . . rise and stand upon your feet; for I have appeared to you for this purpose, to appoint you to serve and bear witness to the things in which you have seen me and to those in which I will appear to you. . . ." (ACTS 26:16) The Risen Lord came to Paul to commission him to work. The Damascus road experience was no end in itself.

Specifically, Paul's commission was to proclaim the news of Jesus Christ not just to his own kind, the Jews, but to outsiders, to despised

173

Gentiles. "I send you," the Living Lord commanded, "to open their eyes, that they may turn from darkness to light and from the power of Satan to God, that they may receive forgiveness of sins and a place among those who are sanctified by faith in me" (ACTS 26:17-18). Gentiles were to be offered forgiveness and a standing in God's community—on the same footing as Jews!

Although many years had elapsed since this order, and although Paul was relating the experience to a smirking Agrippa, Paul's eyes and voice expressed the wonder he first felt when he heard Christ's commission. No dead prophet could have sent him on such an improbable venture, Paul insisted.

Jesus still does what no dead man can do.

In the village of Hueihai in Laos, there is a small, struggling hospital named after Thomas Dooley, the selfless St. Louis doctor who dramatically forsook a lucrative practice to bring healing in the Laotian jungles. Until his untimely death from cancer a few years ago, the hospital thrived. The dynamic Dooley, seizing the imagination of thousands, attracted money, materials, volunteers. After his death, however, the movement lost its impetus. Without Dooley's drive and imagination, the hospital has faltered, and today is seriously understaffed. The Tom Dooley Hospital throbbed with life, as long as its founder was alive.

Compare this to what Jesus has begun. The outreach program of the church, the mission to "Gentiles" in every culture, every continent, throbs with life because the Founder is alive!

Jesus alive? Raised from the dead? Bringing light not only to Jews but to Gentiles, to Romans including Festus? Festus snorted, saying with a loud voice, "Paul, you are mad; your great learning is turning you mad." (ACTS 26:24)

"I am not mad, most excellent Festus, but I am speaking the sober truth." (ACTS 26:25) Paul's reply was fervent because of his experience, not because of "learning." First-hand knowledge of Jesus Christ is different from second-hand information, Paul declared.

Turning to Agrippa, Paul earnestly addressed his plea to the king: "King Agrippa, do you believe the prophets? I know that you believe." (ACTS 26:27)

Agrippa until this point had been enjoying Paul's presentation as he might have followed a stimulating Greek play. Suddenly he realized that he was personally involved in the drama, that he was being pushed into making a personal response. Not wanting to commit himself to anything except his own comfort, Agrippa shook off Paul's challenge. With frosty disdain, the petty king refused any allegiance to the King of kings. "In a short time you think to make me a Christian!" Agrippa answers sarcastically. (ACTS 26:28)

There was no wistfulness in Agrippa's voice, contrary to the suggestion in the King James translation of this verse—"Almost thou persuadest me to be a Christian."

Ignoring Agrippa's haughty reply, Paul gracefully answered, "Whether short or long, I would to God that not only you but also all who hear me this day might become such as I am—" then, with a saving touch of humor and humility, "except for these chains!" (ACTS 26:29)

In spite of the smiles that acknowledged Paul's afterthought, Agrippa had had enough. He rose, signalling that the interview was over and the audience dismissed.

Strengthened by the Spirit, Paul had confronted a king with the Christ. As Paul's valedictory address in Acts, it was fitting that his words be aimed at a man of power and authority.

The words still ring, like priceless crystal, with clear tones of the meaning of Jesus Christ in life. A model sermon even for preachers today, it concludes with a direct appeal for personal decision about Jesus.

Luke wrote Acts for "Theophilus." Remembering that Theophilus was perhaps a governmental official, we notice that Luke goes out of his way to show that even Agrippa and Festus believed Paul to be innocent, agreeing that ". . . this man is doing nothing to deserve death or imprisonment." (ACTS 26:31) Possibly Luke was quietly reminding Theophilus that Christians were not dangerous subversives as rumored, and was bolstering his case by quoting two officials who had interviewed Paul at length. To clinch his case, Luke states that Agrippa added, as an ironical afterthought, "This man could have been set free if he had not appealed to Caesar." (ACTS 26:32)

25

"AND SO WE CAME TO ROME"

(ACTS 27:1-44; 28:1-16)

THAT TORTURED GENIUS, LAWRENCE OF ARABIA, TRIED TO RETIRE from sight after World War I. Exhausted by the rigors of his desert campaign, burned out by the fires of controversy over Arab nationalism, he sought anonymity by enlisting in the R.A.F. as a private, using the name John Hume Ross. Aircraftman Ross, however, was discovered by the London papers to be the famous Colonel Lawrence and subjected to unwanted publicity. Still craving obscurity, Lawrence changed his name again and joined the Royal Tank Corps as T. E. Shaw. Near his camp he rented an old, unused cottage which he made his home. Over the door, Lawrence inscribed the words in Greek which reflected his inner thoughts, "WHAT CARE I?"

After all that Paul had gone through, we would expect such a weary sigh from him. The Apostle, we must remember, had plunged through approximately ten years of grueling travel to organize new congregations (assuming that his first missionary journey was about A.D. 46). After the emotionally and physically exhausting ordeal described in part in Acts, he suffered imprisonment at Caesarea for another two years. Paul, by this time middle-aged, not in robust health, trapped by the intrigues of Roman and Jerusalem temple officials, did not try to crawl away into obscurity. Even during gale and shipwreck on his way to Rome, as described dramatically in ACTS 27, Paul refused to quit.

The human way, after taking so much, is to lie down, thinking, "What care I?" The Spirit's presence means knowing personally that God says, *"I care!"* The Holy Spirit puts yeasty will into tired, depressed men. Through His empowering life, men who should, by all the norms of human existence, give up caring about anyone or anything insist, "I care about others, I care about my own responsibilities."

This was Paul!

Luke and Aristarchus, a Christian from Thessalonica, accompanied Paul on the fateful voyage to Rome. Paul was part of a contingent of prisoners under the charge of one Julian, a considerate centurion of the Augustan Cohort, an elite corps used for military police and confidential errands.

The first port of call was Sidon, seventy sea miles from Caesarea. The centurion thoughtfully permitted Paul to go ashore ". . . to go to his friends and be cared for." (ACTS 27:3) The Greek word, "to be cared for," is a medical term for looking after a sick man, suggesting that Paul was ill. Luke probably advised Paul to get the rest, diet, and medication in a home on shore that he could not get on board a crowded coastal vessel. The ship, meanwhile, laid over at Sidon, taking on or discharging cargo, and perhaps taking on additional prisoners.

The party sailed from Sidon early in the fall, cutting it very close to be in Rome before the end of the shipping season. From mid-September until early November, it was risky to attempt any voyage; from about November eleventh until March fifth, all sea traffic stopped. Luke, following Paul's habit of figuring dates by the Jewish calendar, mentions that "the fast"—or Yom Kippur, the Day of Atonement—had already passed (ACTS 27:9), putting the voyage in the dangerous October-November period.

Usually, ships sailing to Italy from the eastern Mediterranean set a direct course for Sicily and passed to the south of Cyprus. By the time Paul's party sailed, the winds had already begun their seasonal shift. The prevailing winds, from West North West, made a direct tack to Sicily out of the question. For a ship heading toward Italy, these winds meant sailing almost directly into the wind. Racing yachts, cutters, sloops, yawls, schooners, and other craft with a fore-and-aft rig can sail within about six points of the wind. Roman ships, clumsy single-masted, square-rigged vessels, did not dare to sail closer than eight points, and usually preferred to rig one huge yardarm supporting an enormous mainsail and run before the wind.

Upsetting the schedule, unfavorable winds forced Paul's ship to make a long detour north. It beat up to the coast of what is now Turkey, then had to creep from port to port until it finally put in at Myra. It was growing dangerously late to continue the trip. Julius the centurion, however, was anxious to get his charges to Rome. Transferring to an Alexandrian grain ship, one of the fleet that plied from Rome's "breadbasket" in Egypt to Italy, the party pressed on.

When the grain ship rounded the cape at Cnidus, it lost the advantage of the current pushing it, left relatively smooth waters, and ran directly into the prevailing wind and plunged into head waters. The only alternative was to take a starboard tack and run down southward. Instead of following the usual sea lane north of Crete, Paul's ship was forced to stand south of the island. It raised the east tip of Crete, Cape Salmone, and hunted a harbor.

Sailing leeward of Crete, however, brought false hopes among the ship's officers. Lulled into thinking the rest of the passage to Sicily would be like that on the protected side of Crete, a dirty trip, perhaps, but not hazardous, they prepared to stop at Fair Havens, Crete, only long enough to take on supplies.

Paul knew better. An experienced sailor and a veteran of several shipwrecks (II CORINTHIANS 11:25), Paul advised, "Sirs, I perceive that the voyage will be with injury and much loss, not only of the cargo and the ship, but also of our lives." (ACTS 27:10)

The pilot and skipper wanted to continue (not "the captain and the owner" as in the RSV; the words in Greek refer to those in command, not the owner. Besides, Roman grain ships were usually owned by the imperial government.) It was expensive to lay up in harbor for three or four months, paying an idle crew. No officer likes to be accused of being timid. Carrying grain to Rome, especially toward the end of the season, brought a touch of glory. Furthermore, losses were usually covered by the Emperor. Most important, Fair Havens, they insisted, was not suitable to winter in. Ignoring Paul's advice, they made plans to weigh anchor, saying that they could always lay up at Phoenix, a better harbor forty miles farther down the coast.

The difficulty in rounding Cape Matala, a few miles away, should have warned the ship's officers of what lay ahead on more exposed water. Leaving the protection of the land, they found the wind and rain smashing at them with gale force. Forced to alter course, they beat to the south in order to gain the protection of a five-mile-wide speck of island known as Cauda, twenty-three miles off the Crete coast.

Like a fragile pod rolled in the palms of a great, primeval giant, the helpless ship was twisted and pummelled by the gale-churned seas. Grain ships were hefty affairs displacing anywhere from 500 to 1100 tons. One huge mast carrying the great sail concentrated the strain, however, on one part of the hull instead of distributing it. In any violent storm, this meant that there was a tendency for planks to start and leaks to develop. The hull might even split.

Part of the equipment on every ship at that time, as archaeologists

179

point out, were enormous cables or hawsers called "undergirders" (poorly translated in the RSV by the term "measures," ACTS 27:17). These were passed around the hull under the keel and pulled tight. Several lengths of cable or undergirders wrapped around the ship added support and helped prevent straining the timbers. This procedure, called frapping, was fairly common before the use of iron bolts, plates, and turnbuckles, and was done occasionally as late as the nineteenth century.

The hands managed to frap the ship and haul aboard the small boat towed astern during the voyage past Cauda. Then, lowering the yardarm supporting the great mainsail to keep rigging and sail from being blown away and to take some of the strain off the mast, they undoubtedly rigged a small storm sail or reefed the mainsail to keep some control of the ship's direction. Everyone on board knew it would only be a matter of time until the gale slammed the ship on to the dreaded Syrtis, treacherous sandbars off the African coast between Tripoli and Tunis, the final resting place for hundreds of ships and seamen. Desperately trying to turn into the wind to avoid taking the mountainous swells broadside, frantically trying to secure the weakening ship, the sailors began to suspect that the hungry sea would devour one more victim.

Day after day, the storm raged. The crew jettisoned some of the cargo, later threw overboard baggage and extra gear on the decks to lighten the ship and keep it from taking on so much water. Sleeping and eating were impossible. The pumps were useless. Waves continued to wash over the gunwales. Exhausted men, numbed with wet and cold, strained to keep the ship "laid to"—pointed into the wind as much as possible to avoid being caught in the murderous troughs between the waves or being piled up on the coast of Africa. Adding to the problem was the frightening fact that no one had any idea of the ship's position. There was, of course, no compass, no chronometer, no sextant, no reflecting quadrant, no nautical instrument (apart from a crude quadrant held in the hand). "Neither sun nor stars appeared for many a day . . ." Luke reports (ACTS 27:20), so that they had no means whatsoever of reckoning their position.

Luke adds the ominous words, "All hope of our being saved was at last abandoned," (ACTS 27:20)

Illustrating the imperturbability of most seamen, someone recounts an amusing story of an uneasy passenger asking the captain during a squall, "Are we in danger?" "No, ma'm," answered the captain. "The sailors are still swearing. Don't need to worry 'til they start praying."

The phlegmatic hard-bitten sailors on Paul's voyage reached the point where they stopped swearing. Fear, strain, confusion, cold, wet, and hunger ganged up to stamp out all hope. It was only a question of time, they were certain, before the ship would founder.

Every crisis brings out the heroes and the cowards in a community. A man's real strengths and weaknesses are revealed most clearly in times of stress. On a foundering grain ship in the midst of a raging fall gale, the hero with real strength turned out to be a little bandy-legged Jewish-born preacher wearing prisoners' chains.

"Men, you should have listened to me, and should not have set sail from Crete and incurred this injury and loss," he shouted, reminding them of his earlier warnings and qualifying himself as one to be heeded. "I now bid you take heart; for there will be no loss of life among you, but only of the ship. For this very night there stood by me an angel of the God to whom I belong and whom I worship, and he said, 'Do not be afraid, Paul; you must stand before Caesar; and lo, God has granted all those who sail with you.' So take heart, men, for I have faith in God that it will be exactly as I have been told." (ACTS 27:21-25)

It seems incongruous to hear this landlubber telling seamen not to be afraid! They "knew" the sea, understood the promise of watery death in such a maelstrom. Paul, however, knew his Lord, understood *His* promise.

Luke reminds us that God does not remove us from storms or shipwrecks in life. The Spirit assures us that God stands by us in times when everyone is ready to panic.

Fourteen nights after the beginning of the storm and 480 miles after passing Cauda, the sailors heard the unmistakable sound of the crash of surf. After taking soundings which confirmed that they were nearing land, the crew threw out four anchors to hold the lumbering ship until daybreak.

People do strange, unpredictable things in crises, and the crew, cracking after prolonged strain, decided to abandon ship. On the pretext of rowing ahead with a bow anchor, they scurried to launch the boat. Their scheme even fooled Julius the centurion and the ship's officers.

It was Paul who was alert. Warning Julius of the plot, Paul averted disaster. Julius' soldiers chopped away the boat, forcing the sailors to stay with the ship. As the 276 humans on board the leaking, listing ship stood in the lashing rain, peering through the dawn at the thundering breakers, it seemed useless to try anything. Once again, it was

Paul's faith and common sense that saved the group. Pointing out that they were all weak from constant suspense and hunger, Paul encouraged them to pull themselves together by eating something, then set the example by taking bread, giving thanks to God publicly for it, and having a hearty breakfast.

Paul, the only calm, thinking and confident man in the entire company, was the only man who kept his head in the emergency. The others, despairing, had literally stopped eating.

Psychiatrists studying the effects of prison camps on various persons have pointed out that there is a close connection between faith and eating. During the Korean War, for instance, there were dozens of well-documented examples of young P.O.W.'s in the prime of life and without wounds or disease who simply allowed themselves to be overcome with despair and gave up. Curled up in a hut, these boys quit eating, finding it too much effort to try to survive, and usually died within three or four weeks.

On the other hand, the man of faith has a motive for keeping alive. His motive for wanting to live means that he finds methods for staying alive. Unexpected powers of creativity and endurance are released by the Holy Spirit, as countless veterans of death-camps can testify.

Paul helped the others to stand up in the crisis. After eating, they all went to work to heave the cargo overboard.

Soaked with salt, it was useless. Worse, the grain had shifted to the port side after the ship had heeled for so many days on the starboard tack, making the ship list dangerously. The plan was to trim and lighten the ship so that she would ride as high in the water as possible. Lashing the two paddle-rudders on the deck, they hoisted a foresail and headed the hulk for the beach.

The weary ship, however, rammed into a mudbank offshore. Stuck fast and pounded by the surf, it began to break up.

The soldiers, answerable with their lives if their prisoners escaped, unbuckled their broadswords. Businesslike, they prepared to butcher the entire lot. Mostly out of respect for prisoner Paul, Julius ordered his troopers to put away their swords and told everyone to try to save himself.

Safely on shore, the shivering survivors huddled around a fire and discovered that they were on Malta. Most were in semi-shock, standing helplessly. Paul, as usual, seemed to know what to do. Busy and helpful, he gathered firewood. While he was carrying a load of brush toward the fire, a viper sluggishly came out of the brush and wrapped itself around Paul's hand. Paul casually shook the thing into the fire. The natives, assuming that Paul's manacles meant that he was a criminal, waited for him to collapse from snakebite as divine punishment for his apparent misdeeds. When Paul appeared unharmed, the Maltese acclaimed him as someone divine.

The island of Malta today proudly identifies the landing place of the shipwrecked party that bleak dawn as "St. Paul's Bay." Although Luke does not specifically say, the Maltese also insist that Paul founded the church on their island. Luke does state, however, that he and Paul carried on an intensive ministry during their stay on Malta. A hearty paganism is a better climate for evangelism than a dishonest piety, and Malta warmly received Paul's and Luke's efforts.

Paul and Luke at Malta were the first medical missionaries. Discovering that the father of the island's head man, Publius, was ill from fever and dysentery, they healed him. Later, the other sick of Malta ". . . came and were cured" (ACTS 28:9), or as Luke's precise clinical term in the Greek literally means, "received medical treatment." Notice that it was not prayer only or medicine only, but both! Paul and Luke, pastor and physician, worked as a healing team. Their ministry could best be summed up by that famous inscription over the door of the ancient Paris hospital: "I only dressed his wounds, God healed him."

After three months on Malta, centurion Julius ordered his party aboard a ship for Sicily. The stormy season was ending.

Tradition holds that Paul also founded the church at Sicily, but Luke mentions only a three-day layover at Syracuse. Leaving Sicily, they crossed to the mainland, landing briefly at Rhegium on the tip of the boot of Italy, then re-embarking for the last leg of the voyage to Puteoli in the lovely Bay of Naples.

Julius held his troop at Puteoli while he sent his report ahead to Rome and waited for orders. Paul, Aristarchus, and Luke, meanwhile, were entertained by Christians at Puteoli. Word was carried to the Christian community at Rome that Paul had landed.

Any uneasiness that Paul had had about how he would be received by the church at Rome was quickly dispelled. As the weary, haggard Apostle in chains trudged toward Rome, he was gladdened by reception committees of cordial Christians. One party tramped all the way down to the Forum of Appius, the transportation hub forty-three miles south of Rome. Another joined the procession at the Three Taverns, thirty-three miles from Rome on the Appian Way. Luke records the deep emotions at these meetings: "On seeing them, Paul thanked God and took courage." (ACTS 28:15) Paul, who had supported so many others in their loneliness and fear, was for once supported by others. The church in Italy, ministering to the Apostle, demonstrated that its love was genuine.

With two contingents of welcoming Christians accompanying him, the old saint's arrival at Rome took on the air of a triumphal entry in spite of the chains. This promise of the Spirit was fulfilled—Paul actually came to the Imperial City!

26

THE NARRATIVE WHICH
HAS NO ENDING

(ACTS 28:17-31)

CHAINED TO A GUARD, THE DOUGHTY OLD APOSTLE AND HIS TWO lieutenants, Luke and Aristarchus, had at last arrived at Rome. Although the Imperial City, with its population of over two million, was unrivalled for nearly two thousand years (as late as the sixteenth century, even London was a dingy place of only about twelve thousand), Paul cared nothing about the splendor or the sights.

Three days after arriving, Paul, still experiencing heartbreak because his own people did not know the news of Jesus Christ, called together the leaders of the synagogues at Rome. Briefly outlining his case, the missionary in manacles requested an audience with the Jewish community in the capital, explaining ". . . it is because of the hope of Israel that I am bound with this chain." (ACTS 28:20)

Word had not yet reached Rome's synagogues of the ruckus over Paul at Jerusalem and Caesarea. The leaders agreed and set a date for Paul to make his presentation.

Earnest though Paul was, he did not convince everyone. After a day-long seminar of ". . . testifying to the kingdom of God and trying to convince them about Jesus both from the law of Moses and from the prophets." (ACTS 28:23) Paul was struck by the similarity between his own time and the way so many in ancient Israel had rejected the prophets' message. The Apostle thereupon recited an apt selection—the most quoted Old Testament passage in the New Testament—from ISAIAH 6:9-10, in which the prophet reminds his people that they do not really want to listen or see what God has done.

It seems fitting that the last mention of Paul in Acts should show him still addressing his own people, the Jews, on the meaning of the gospel. His last recorded words in Acts are a summary of his ministry, "Let it be known to you then that this salvation of God has been sent to the Gentiles; they will listen." (ACTS 28:28)

There are only two remaining verses in the entire Book of Acts: "And he lived there two whole years at his own expense, and welcomed all who came to him, preaching the kingdom of God and teaching about the Lord Jesus Christ quite openly and unhindered." (ACTS 28:30-31) The narrative abruptly stops. One almost suspects that someone has ripped out some pages—the story breaks off so suddenly that it seems that there must be more. What happened to Paul?

We must remind ourselves that Luke is not writing so much about Paul as about the work of the Holy Spirit. Because of the Spirit, the gospel was preached at the hub of world, "openly and unhindered." Luke has completed his sweeping survey of how the Spirit, starting at Jerusalem with a handful in the Upper Room, has propelled members of the Spirit-filled community everywhere, even to Rome itself. His narrative of the acts of the Holy Spirit can be concluded. The gospel is being preached at Rome!

Why was Paul's case allowed to drag on for two years or more? Long delays in trials were common in the first century. Historians recount many cases where defendants were detained for years before their cases were resolved.

One reason why Paul's hearing was postponed for so long was that the records from Festus at Caesarea were lost in the wreck at Malta. It would take months for a new transcript of the previous proceedings in Palestine to reach Rome. It was also necessary for accusers to appear in person at a Roman trial. Possibly the Jerusalem priests sent to bring charges against deposed governor Felix were also appointed to prosecute Paul. With shipping on the Mediterranean at a standstill about five months each year, and with the problem of gathering key witnesses from Syria, Macedonia, Asia Minor, and Greece as well as Judea to appear against Paul, preparation for a trial could easily drag out over two years. Moreover, Nero and his Roman henchmen, never liking to be bothered with the welfare of citizens, often procrastinated in hearing appeals.

During those two years, however, Paul was not idle. In spite of being chained constantly to a Roman soldier, he energetically did everything possible to promote the gospel. He found time to meet with a procession of fascinating church members, including John Mark, with whom he had the memorable falling-out years earlier during the first mission tour with Barnabas, but with whom he became completely reconciled. Respected by the rough young troopers around the barracks, the aging Apostle sat long hours presenting the meaning of Jesus Christ to various members of the Praetorian Guard. Eventually, there were converts even in "Caesar's household." (PHILIPPIANS 4:22)

Since last rounding his circuit of churches, Paul had heard of many problems confronting them. He, of course, was not able to visit them. He could, however, receive committees or emissaries from these congregations and send back advice. Occasionally, the missionary dashed off a letter, dictating it to one of his friends attending him since his manacles made it nearly impossible for him to write. Today, some of Paul's prison correspondence from this period at Rome—Ephesians, Philippians, Colossians, and Philemon—are priceless parts of our New Testament canon. Were it not for Paul's imprisonment and the epistles fired off as a result, our Bible would be considerably slimmer and our insights into the gospel considerably thinner!

What finally became of Paul? Although Luke leaves us hanging, we can fill in the gaps by some detective work in reading the prison letters and early historians.

The evidence is overwhelming that the old missionary made one final tour after being imprisoned at Rome for two years. Whether his case was settled or postponed after a preliminary hearing, we cannot be certain. Nearly all ancient authorities—Clement of Rome, Eusebius, Chrysostom, and Jerome—agree that Paul even journeyed to the extreme west, undoubtedly Spain, as well as Dalmatia, Macedonia, Crete, Ephesus, Miletus, and Nicopolis.

Somewhere, somehow, Paul was re-arrested and brought back to Rome a second time. Tradition maintains that this was shortly after the Great Fire which levelled Rome in July, A.D. 64, when Nero needed scapegoats.

During the second imprisonment at Rome the weary, aged saint penned the Pastoral Epistles—I and II Timothy and Titus. He knew that his days were numbered, suspected that he would never be released but would be executed in Nero's bloodbath. Aching from the effects of years of privation and lonely for companionship, Paul unburdened himself to Timothy.

What did he write in such bleak conditions?

George Washington in the dismal winter of 1776, faltering as cold and hunger seemed about to put out the last sparks of hope in his starving camp, wrote a soul-baring letter to his brother, John Augustine. Dated December 18, 1776, the letter reads, "I think the game is pretty near up . . . no man, I believe, ever had a greater choice of difficulties and less means to extricate himself from them. . . ."

No "game-is-up" groan from the Spirit-supported Apostle. "The Lord will rescue me from every evil," he stoutly avowed, "and save me for his heavenly kingdom." (II TIMOTHY 4:18) This was his last communication.

He was beheaded with a sword outside the gates of Rome on the road to Ostia, A.D. 64.

Luke omits these details, probably because to him they were not really important. The vital matter was that the Holy Spirit was still at work in His church.

We have already noted that Luke might originally have contemplated a third volume to follow his Gospel account and Acts. Some scholars, in fact, explain the abrupt ending of Acts by saying that Luke planned to continue his narrative of Paul's work and the growth of the church in another book. So far as we know, this final volume to the projected trilogy was never written.

In a sense, however, another volume is now being written. The Holy Spirit is still at work. The story of the church is a narrative that has no ending. The community of Spirit-filled men and women is still witnessing to the gospel of Jesus Christ.

Many of the Acts of the Spirit in our generation are unheralded, even unknown. In Asia, for example, men and women are making incredible sacrifices for "the Way" in their own remote villages.

"You shall be my witnesses," Luke records Jesus as commanding his followers after the resurrection. (ACTS 1:8) Given the promise of the Holy Spirit, we are sent as His witnesses. We are responsible for today's installment of the narrative that has no ending. We have been welded by the Holy Spirit into a community which is called to witness to *The* Act of God!